Get Set for Politics

WITHDRAWN

Titles in the GET SET FOR UNIVERSITY series:

Get Set for American Studies
ISBN 0 7486 1692 6

Get Set for English Language
ISBN 0 7486 1544 X

Get Set for English Literature
ISBN 0 7486 1537 7

Get Set for Geography
ISBN 0 7486 1693 4

Get Set for Linguistics
ISBN 0 7486 1694 2

Get Set for Media Studies
ISBN 0 7486 1695 0

Get Set for Philosophy
ISBN 0 7486 1657 8

Get Set for Politics
ISBN 0 7486 1545 8

Get Set for Study in the UK
ISBN 0 7486 1810 4

Get Set for Politics

Keith Faulks, Ken Phillips and Alex Thomson

Edinburgh University Press

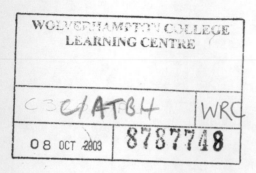
© Keith Faulks, Ken Phillips and Alex Thomson, 2003

Edinburgh University Press Ltd
22 George Square, Edinburgh

Typeset in Sabon
by Hewer Text Ltd, Edinburgh, and
printed and bound in Finland by
WS Bookwell

A CIP record for this book is
available from the British Library

ISBN 0 7486 1545 8 (paperback)

CONTENTS

INTRODUCTION

Now, more than ever before, human beings need politics. Pick up a newspaper or turn on the television and we are constantly made aware of the violent consequences of the breakdown of political dialogue, whether it be in Afghanistan, the Middle East, the Balkans or Northern Ireland. Disputes between different belief systems or cultures are nothing new of course, but the need to find political solutions to our problems is now more acute because we live in an era when technological advances have produced readily available weapons of mass destruction. Today, the potential is always there for conflict to escalate to the point where the planet itself is in peril.

We also live in an age where in a growing number of countries citizens are able to participate in their own govern-ance through the workings of democracy. Many of us have the opportunity to collectively choose what services the state should provide and how much we should pay for these. Citizens need to make *informed* choices if this system of democracy is to work effectively.

The study of politics is therefore more relevant than ever. Civilisation itself requires humans to increase their knowledge of why conflicts arise and to search for appropriate methods of conflict resolution. Similarly, democracy demands that in-creasingly more efficient institutions and policies are designed to allocate resources throughout society. Politics provides many of the solutions to these problems. Above all, it is the way in which humans avoid clashes of interest being resolved by the knife, the bullet or the ballistic missile.

You are to be congratulated, then, for being prepared to take such issues seriously by choosing to study politics your-self. By doing this you are bucking a worrying trend. Many people, particularly in Western societies, are increasingly

becoming turned off politics altogether. There is a deep cynicism with regard to politicians and political parties, as witnessed by the falling turnout in many local and national
elections.

The aim of this book is, in a very modest way, to help you
swim against this tide of cynicism. While its main audience will
be students who have enrolled or are considering enrolling on
a Politics course at university, its subject matter will be of
interest to those taking GCSE or A level Politics, or even those
who have no intention of studying politics formally but want a
quick guide to what the subject is all about.

THE STRUCTURE OF THE BOOK

Get Set for Politics is organised into three parts. In Part I we
look first at how politics might best be defined. You will find
that there is a great deal of debate about exactly what politics
is and so Chapter 1 looks at some competing approaches and
possible alternative to politics. The second chapter introduces
two concepts, power and the state, that are central to the study
of politics. In Chapter 3, we take a look at how Politics has
developed as an academic discipline and ask whether the
subject can justifiably be called a science.

Part II looks in more detail at the content of a typical degree
programme in Politics. In our own teaching we have found it
useful to divide the study of Politics into three main sub-
disciplines and so this part of the book is organised into three
chapters covering each of these in turn. Chapter 4 is concerned
with Political Theory and looks at the great thinkers, concepts
and ideologies that have provided the framework for both
practical and academic political activity. The next chapter
tackles Government, exploring how political scientists study
governmental institutions such as the state and political participation such as voting and protesting. The final chapter in
Part II turns its attention to the international aspects of
politics, examining how scholars have tried to explain the
roots of global conflict and inequality.

Having analysed the nature and content of Politics in the first two parts of the book, Part III attempts to equip you with some useful skills by which you can better study the subject. Chapter 7 looks specifically at study skills that you will find invaluable in the formal study of the discipline: you will learn more and quicker if you consciously seek to improve your techniques of writing, computing and presenting. The final chapter of the book aims to get you thinking about how the skills you are developing whilst studying Politics can be useful in the world of work and for enhancing your life generally.

Throughout the book, we have tried to avoid unnecessary jargon and instead aim to provide you with a readable over-view of politics in all its aspects. It is important to stress, however, that a book such as this can barely scratch the surface of what is a huge subject. If we do enough to encourage you to enquire further into Politics, then we have achieved our main objective. With this in mind, each chapter concludes with a short guide to further reading which we encourage you to follow up. Also, given we are covering so much ground and have therefore not been able to define every term we have discussed within the main text, we thought it would be useful to conclude the book with a glossary of brief, but hopefully not too superficial, definitions of some key concepts. These terms appear in bold in the main text.

ON BECOMING A POLITICS STUDENT

For those of you who do intend taking Politics at university, whether on its own or in combination with other subjects, here are a few useful tips to start you off:

Approach your studies with an open mind. Studying Politics inevitably entails challenging some deep-seated beliefs you may have about the world. These beliefs may not change but you should by the end of your studies be able to express more clearly and logically why you believe what you do.

Take an active interest in current affairs. A quality newspaper is an invaluable source for Politics students and you should subscribe to one if you are serious about your subject. Look out also for the many excellent television programmes such as *Question Time, Channel Four News, Newsnight* and *On the Record* which help bring politics to life.

Become computer literate. If you cannot operate a personal computer, now is the time to learn! The World Wide Web, word processing and statistical packages are just three good reasons why any serious student of Politics needs to know their way around a computer.

Buy a Politics dictionary. The purchase of a good politics dictionary early on in your studies is a very sensible move. Having one to hand at all times will greatly aid your understanding of the often complex materials you will be studying. Chapter 7 gives some examples of such dictionaries but if you are to buy just one we recommend Roger Scruton's (1996) *Dictionary of Political Thought,* which provides a multitude of pithy and entertaining definitions of political terms.

Finally, we hope you enjoy the book and good luck with your studies!

PART I
Defining Politics

Keith Faulks

1 WHAT IS POLITICS?

Politics should matter to us all because it is concerned with fundamental questions that are of profound relevance to human beings, whenever or wherever they may live: How can we live in peace? Why are millions of people in some parts of the world dying of hunger? What **rights** should I be entitled to? How can I make my voice heard? Why should I obey the government? What should be the limits, if any, to my personal freedom? These are just some of the important issues you will be exploring if you choose to take your interest in politics further.

It is because the study of politics addresses such important dilemmas that Aristotle (384–322 BC) (1962), one of the first thinkers to study the subject systematically, argued that it was the 'master science'. Aristotle did not think it was enough merely to study politics, however. He felt that it was the duty of all rational beings (he did not include women, but we shall come to that later) to engage in political activity themselves. Human beings were, for Aristotle, by nature 'political animals'. To seek to avoid participation in politics meant that one must be either 'a beast or a God'. Not all those who have studied politics share such a positive view. In a class of mine a few years ago, a student replied to Aristotle's challenge by stating that being either a beast or a God sounded pretty good to him! An amusing comment, but nevertheless indicative of a widespread cynicism that exists about the merits of politics today – even amongst some students of the subject! We are assuming that as you are reading this book, and perhaps thinking about studying politics in more depth yourself, you are at the very least open to persuasion about the merits of taking politics seriously. Any beasts or Gods still with us can, of course, stop reading at this point.

One of the most fascinating and, at times, frustrating aspects of studying politics is that the nature of the concept is itself highly controversial. No one can seem to agree what politics actually is or what purpose it serves. If you have chosen to read Politics at college or university you will undoubtedly find a fair proportion of your time will be devoted to trying to define the subject you are studying. What is more, you will be drawing upon a range of other disciplines as diverse as History, Philosophy, Sociology, Economics, Psychology, Anthropology and Geography in order to comprehend the nature of political activity.

It is important to remember there are no right answers to the question 'What is politics?' This chapter does not therefore seek to furnish you with a single neat definition of the subject. Instead, what it aims to do is get you thinking critically about what the study of politics entails. First, we shall begin by looking at the origins of politics: what problems does politics aim to solve? Second, we shall explore some influential inter-pretations of what politics does and/or should mean. Finally, we examine whether there can be practical alternatives to oganising societies through political decision-making.

THE ORIGINS OF POLITICS

The need for politics arises from the fact that, as the German philosopher Karl Marx once observed, human beings are social animals. People generally choose to live in communities with others rather than as hermits. Given this, all human communities of whatever size are faced with two fundamental and inherent challenges:

1. *How can we live together in harmony, without resort to violence?*
Amongst all the numerous species that inhabit planet Earth, human beings have a unique level of consciousness. This allows them to construct models or theories about the nature of the world that they see around them. Some have turned to religious explanations, accounting for the origins and nature of life by worshipping an unseen consciousness higher than that of humankind. Others think the world is best explained

through scientific enquiry, driven by reason rather than faith. Within these broad religious and scientific approaches there are countless varieties of perspectives, beliefs and ideas. The important point for us, in the context of trying to understand why we have politics, is that individuals have widely different interpretations of the world around them.

When individuals who see the world differently live together in the same community, or have to interact with other communities, the potential for conflict exists. It is important to distinguish between positive conflict and negative conflict, however. Because people have diverse value systems, argument, debate and deliberation are inevitable. This can be highly positive, as new ideas that take human understanding forward are often generated through the synthesis of previously opposed ideas. Conflict becomes negative when differences lead to the breakdown of debate, and communities or individuals resort to violence in order to attempt to resolve their disputes with others.

Differences between people's value systems mean, then, that communities face the task of attempting to maintain social order. This problem is closely linked to a second major challenge that all human communities face:

2. *How should we distribute the resources upon which our lives depend?*
We are, of course, physical creatures who require sustenance and shelter. This means that all communities have to find ways to produce and distribute the resources that ensure that the basic needs of its members are met. Resources are, however, in most cases finite. This means that some needs go unfulfilled. Some communities will lack access to certain raw materials, for example, and this may lead to scarcity, famine and poverty. Indeed, perhaps the major cause of violent conflicts both within and between communities is the struggle for the control of resources. To give an example from World War II, one of Japan's main reasons for attacking the Americans at Pearl Harbor in 1941 was the Japanese's lack of access to important raw materials such as oil. The Japanese felt that by crippling the navy of their biggest rival in the Pacific they would be able to buy

time in order to allow themselves to build an empire in South East Asia and this would help solve their resource problems.

The issue of resource distribution is invariably connected to the problem of value conflicts identified earlier. The way that people understand the world will influence how they approach the question of resources. Some communities may feel that the prejudices of others mean that they have been treated unfairly and denied access to resources. To take our example of Japan's actions in the Second World War, at the heart of Japan's military expansionism was a deep-seated sense of grievance against the West. Japan felt that countries like Britain and America had shaped the world economic system in such a way as to deny countries like Japan fair access to trade. This was attributed in large part to racism on the part of the West. These kinds of conflict exist not just *between* communities but *within* them as well. Many of the issues that concern students of politics are to do with how we can obtain a just distribution of resources within a particular society and why in practice this is rarely, if ever, achieved.

It is, then, questions of social order and the distribution of resources that generate the need for politics. At its broadest level, the practice of politics is an attempt to resolve these two related and inherent human problems. If we understand politics in this way it is obvious that *all* human communities, both past, present and future, are political communities. This view challenges the commonly held assumption that only modern **states**, with highly sophisticated systems of government and rule, can be called political.

As Schedler (1997: 3) notes, 'politics delineates the realm of common affairs'. As long as human beings live in interdependent relationships with other individuals and, importantly, they recognise that their existence is interdependent with that of other people, then politics is a necessary and fundamental human activity. This is the case regardless of the size or complexity of the community under consideration. In her study of stateless societies, the anthropologist Lucy Mair (1962) shows how relatively 'primitive' communities nonetheless have institutions and practices that seek to resolve conflicts through the systematic making and enforcement of rules: the methods of rule used may differ but politics is an ever-present feature of human communities. As we shall see later, attempts to solve the problems of order and resources through non-political means invariably involves bringing politics in through the back door.

Having identified why we need politics, we need now to turn to exploring a few of the numerous ways the concept has been defined.

DEFINING POLITICS

Politics as deliberation and compromise

We have already noted human beings' unique capacity for interpreting and explaining the world. Because politics is concerned with highly charged issues such as how we should best organise our communities and who should get what resources, it is hardly surprising that definitions of politics are themselves highly diverse. Any individual's understanding of what we mean by politics is bound up with their general view of life, their values and their own experience of the world.

One influential view is that politics is concerned with the exchange of opposing views, the ultimate aim of which is the peaceful resolution of conflicts over values and resources. This definition would imply that at the heart of political activity is deliberation and compromise between what might be very different perspectives. It is generally assumed that this communication between opposing perspectives is concerned primarily with 'the definition of societal problems and conflicts' (Schedler 1997: 3). It is then focused upon resolving disputes that occur at a community level rather than those which arise within personal or family relationships. Bernard Crick (2000: 18) expresses this divide concisely when he asserts that: 'Politics are the public actions of free men. Freedom is the privacy of men from public actions.' We see later that not all theorists agree that we can so neatly delineate the public, and therefore the political, from the personal.

The idea of politics as compromise necessarily excludes violence as a legitimate method of asserting one's wishes. Indeed, according to this perspective, the use of violence represents the breakdown or failure of politics. Crick (2000: 18), in a famous defence of this view of politics, summarises its essence by comparing the political method of rule to that of tyranny and oligarchy:

> For politics, as Aristotle points out, is only one possible solution to the problem of order. It is by no means the most usual. Tyranny is the most obvious alternative – the rule of one strong man in his own interest; and oligarchy is the next most obvious alternative – the rule of one group in their own interest. The method of rule of the tyrant and the oligarch is quite simply to clobber, coerce, or overawe all or most of these other groups in the interest of their own. The political method of rule is to listen to these other groups so as to conciliate them as far as possible, and to give them a legal position, a sense of security, some clear and reasonably safe means of articulation, by which these other groups can and will speak freely.

According to this kind of argument, politics can be defined as a set of techniques, including **diplomacy, democracy,** and delib-eration, that aim to resolve conflict over values or resources peacefully. Such a resolution of conflict almost inevitably in-volves compromise on all sides. Importantly, though, politics does not seek to *end* differences but rather to *accommodate* them through a set of agreed principles, rules and regulations. Crick (2000: 21) goes on to summarise this approach as follows:

> Politics, then, can be simply defined as the activity by which differing interests within a given unit of rule are conciliated by giving them a share in power in proportion to their importance to the welfare and survival of the whole community.

Crick draws inspiration from Aristotle's famous view that human beings are, by their nature, political animals. Crick argues that politics, as he defines it, is ennobling to the human spirit because it helps to encourage life-enhancing skills such as empathy for others, consideration and toleration. This view is seen by some as both naïve and too narrow. It is naïve because in the 'real world' a key method of achieving one's goals is the use of violence. It is too narrow because it would appear to apply only to societies that have institutions that are broadly democratic and participatory.

Politics as the 'will to power'

In contrast to the view that politics is about compromise, this approach suggests that politics is no more than the pursuit of **power,** where power is defined as the ability to successfully exercise one's will even where others may be opposed.

This view is perhaps the broadest possible approach to politics. This is firstly because if we accept that power is present in some form in all human relationships, politics could then be said to be concerned with family life and voluntary organisations, as well as more formal 'political' institutions such as governments, parties and pressure groups. It is for this reason that many feminists, concerned with the emancipation of women from the dominance of men, have been attracted by the idea of politics as the pursuit of power. Through the now famous slogan 'the personal is political', feminists have neatly expressed the view that conflicts over values and resources take place in *all* spheres of human life, including the 'private sphere' of the family, and not just in the 'public sphere' in institutions like the workplace or parliaments. Feminists argue that women have often been directly or indirectly excluded from formal institutions of politics because in their private lives men have sought to assert their will at the expense of women's interest. This domination by men very often involves the use of physical violence against women.

This last point brings us to a second reason why defining

politics as the pursuit of power is a very broad way of understanding the concept. The idea of politics as compromise excludes the notion that violence is part of political activity. In fact, violence is seen by writers such as Crick as the antithesis of politics: wherever and whenever deliberation, compromise and democracy fail, violence will result. Alternatively, violence might be seen as just another method by which an individual or group can assert their will.

The Prussian military theorist Clausewitz (1780–1831) (1976: 87) expresses exactly this view when he contends that **war** is 'a true political instrument, a continuation of political activity by other means'. Some dictators have taken this doctrine to its logical extreme. Hitler (1969), for example, argues in *Mein Kampf* that politics is an art concerned with the violent assertion of one's ethnicity, expressed above all through a commitment to one's nation, the 'Fatherland'. A movement like the Nazis in Germany, both before and during World War II, utilised violence as the primary method of politics and all but abandoned any sense of cooperation, compromise and conciliation.

Some theorists have viewed this approach as a more accurate description of political behaviour than seeing politics as the 'art of compromise', because it reflects human nature as it is rather than as we might wish it to be. The German nineteenth-century scholar Friedrich Nietzsche, for example, was of the view that mass movements such as Christianity, **liberalism** or **socialism** have sought to deny individuals their unique identity as power-seeking creatures by falsely defining all people as equal. For Nietzsche, the challenge for the intelligent individual is to reject the erroneous claims of such movements, which attempt to promote universal values and rights for everyone, and instead to make their 'will to power' the purpose of their existence. Politics becomes a method through which the strong assert their supremacy over the weak. Such a view is more cynical but, some would say, more realistic than that expressed by writers like Crick.

The dangers of this perspective are, however, twofold. First, as the example of Nazi Germany illustrates, if humans see violence as a wholly natural and legitimate method of pursuing power, little space will be left for less dramatic forms of politics such as deliberation and dialogue. Second, even where violence does not totally engulf other aspects of political life, politics is discredited in the eyes of the general population because it is hopelessly tainted with its association with naked self-interest pursued by any means necessary. There is no doubt that this is exactly how many feel about politics today.

Politics as a dirty word

In his song *Political World*, Bob Dylan (1989) expresses a widely held opinion about politics in his opening lines:

> We live in a political world, love don't have any place
> We're living in times, when man can make crimes, and
> crime don't have a face.

In the rest of his song, Dylan presents a sustained attack on the 'political world'. Politics is a synonym for evil. Politics is the opposite of love. It is at heart an activity that is cynical, hypocritical and is more often than not a 'respectable' mask behind which hides corruption and secret deals that benefit the powerful but which have little to do with **justice** or the democratic will: the 'crimes that have no face' as Dylan puts it.

This cynical view of what politics is and what it can achieve is undoubtedly a popular one. How often do we read about the need to 'keep politics out' of sport, or family life, or education. How regularly do we complain about office politics? When we are accused of being political in our own lives this is a (relatively) subtle way of saying we are acting in a devious or manipulative fashion.

Such a negative view of political life is given some credence, it is sometimes argued, by the actions of politicians themselves. In societies with free and sophisticated mass media, we are used to seeing politicians being exposed in all their inglorious hypocrisy by the press or television. The last few years of President Clinton's presidency in the USA were dominated by endless debates about his dubious business dealings and his decadent private life. In the UK, the Conservative government of John Major was beset with problems of 'sleaze' ranging from MPs taking cash to ask questions in the House of Commons to sexual impropriety. Such high-profile incidents have helped to create a mood of deep antipathy towards politicians and politics generally.

There are, of course, very worrying consequences that follow from seeing politics primarily as a dirty word. For governments that base their **legitimacy** upon the popular will, it is particularly depressing to see the development of a deep-rooted cynicism towards participation in political institutions. Recent studies of **political participation** in developed states, such as voting turn-out and membership of political parties, have demonstrated an alarming decline in citizens' willingness to actively involve themselves in decision making within their country (Faulks 1999: 148–155). A good example of this was the 2001 British General Election when only 59 per cent of voters were prepared to cast their vote, whereas historically well over 70 per cent have tended to vote in national elections. Especially worrying is that the lowest turnout rates were amongst the eighteen–twenty-four-year old age range, suggesting that for many young people politics is seen, at best, as irrelevant to their lives. The picture is even worse in the USA, with turnout even in presidential elections hovering around 50 per cent in recent years. Countries which pride themselves on being political democracies, such as the USA or UK, are indeed in trouble when politics becomes little more than an insult, a practice associated with meddling, manipulation and malevolence.

The use of politics as a term of abuse is not a recent phenomenon, however. Before the advent of modern political parties in the nineteenth century, a few closely connected families that governed through **faction** dominated Britain's decision making processes. The term politics was applied to such factional groupings in condemnation of their self-interested pursuit of their own, rather than the country's, interests. Even many influential political theorists have themselves been sceptical of the role politics plays in our lives. The whole conservative tradition, for example, could be said to contain a strong anti-political element.

Edmund Burke (1729–97) (1968), one of the most important founders of modern **conservatism,** was highly skeptical of the value of politics. In a famous attack on the **French Revolution** of 1789, Burke argued that abstract political ideas of liberty, **equality** and fraternity were being asserted at the expense of more reliable values associated with the wisdom of the past, such as tradition, piety and hierarchy. Burke believed that governments were rarely capable of pursuing the common good successfully. Conservatives who have been influenced by the ideas of Burke have often stressed this criticism of government. When Margaret Thatcher came to power at the head of a Conservative government in 1979, she made one of her key aims the 'rolling back of the state', allegedly as a way of curtailing the role political decision-making played in Britain's affairs.

It is not only conservative thinkers who have been wary of the perils of 'big government'. The eighteenth-century liberal Thomas Paine (1737–1809), who famously defended the achievements of the French Revolution against Burke, was no less wary of a world dominated by politics. Paine (1995: 5) declared in his book *Common Sense* that 'government even in its best state is but a necessary evil'. Paine does not only share with Burke a general scepticism towards politics; both thinkers are also staunch advocates of the **free market** as a more efficient way than government intervention of distributing resources and ensuring balance within society.

This leads us logically to consider whether, given such cynicism exists towards politics, there is not a better way of resolving successfully the two challenges of order and resources identified at the start of this chapter.

ALTERNATIVES AND CHALLENGES TO POLITICS

The market rules, OK?

The view that the free market is a more effective method than politics of resolving the dilemmas of social order and the distribution of resources is an increasingly influential one. The liberal economist Adam Smith (1723–90) is perhaps the most highly regarded guru of the market creed.

In his famous book, *The Wealth of Nations*, Smith (1976) contends that humans have a natural tendency to barter, trade and exchange goods and services. He also argues that each individual will pursue their own interests in such a way as to maximise their personal wealth. Individual self-interest, balanced by the self-interest of others, expressed through competition between different producers, would ensure an ordered society. Smith uses the metaphor of an 'invisible hand' to explain how the laws of supply and demand ensure that if a need exists someone will seek to meet that need by supplying the relevant product or service. Although the supplier is motivated by *individual* self-interest, the general effect would be the promotion of a *social* good – the satisfaction of a need or want. These 'natural laws' of economics are favourably contrasted with the artificial institutions of political design. Government, because it tends towards defending vested interests, and is by nature bureaucratic and unresponsive to the ever-changing needs of citizens, should play a very limited role. Primarily, Smith asserts government should act to secure order from threats from both within and outside a society.

In the final quarter of the twentieth century, Smith's views were hugely influential in the development of what is often referred to as **neo-liberalism.** Writers such as Nozick and Hayek have reworked Smith's ideas to argue for a minimalist approach to politics and government in favour of a market-orientated solution to social order and the problem of resources. Nozick, for example, talks of the need for a 'night-watchman state', which has as its objective the protection of the basic rights (to life, **liberty** and property) that every individual enjoys by mere fact of being human. All other human interaction should be regulated not through politics but by the free market. Nozick suggests, for example, that taxation, raised by governments to finance their policies, is in fact a form of forced labour.

It is, however, highly doubtful whether the 'free' market can ever fully replace the need for politics. For one thing, many of the differences and debates in society cannot be reduced to economic considerations. Clashes over moral issues such as abortion or gay rights require political debate and the framing of laws informed by that debate. Secondly, markets have always operated within a political context. Even radical advocates of the virtues of the market such as Nozick have to concede that *some* form of government is necessary to ensure order within society. Thirdly, many commentators question whether, given the inequalities that inevitably result from unregulated markets, a society can remain stable. The well-documented relationship between poverty, crime and public disorder illustrates the limits of treating humans as mere economic commodities whose worth is equal only to that of their market value.

Very often, arguments for placing greater emphasis on market solutions rather than political ones are based not just upon the supposed superiority of the market but also the alleged impossibility of ordinary people making sensible political decisions. A good example of this is the work of the neo-liberal Hayek (1944: 122), who as well as arguing strongly for a much greater role for the market also contends that 'probably it is true enough that the great majority are rarely capable of thinking independently'. Such views have been developed into a particular political theory often referred to as **elite theory.**

Decisions by 'experts'

The complexities associated with managing a society's affairs are so great, it could be argued, that decision-making is best left to the experts. Such views have a long history in political theory and have always been used by those elites who seek to limit the realm of politics to themselves.

Elitist arguments are normally of two kinds. Firstly, it is argued that in large-scale societies it is not possible to involve the masses (ordinary people) in decision-making. To try to do this would be impractical and would slow the process of decisions down to almost a standstill. Moreover, highly technical issues of a military, scientific or bureaucratic nature can only be fully understood by those who have dedicated their lives to understanding them. Mass involvement would merely dilute the quality of decisions made by experts. Secondly, many elite theorists have had grave doubts about ordinary people's capacity for rational thought, much less responsible decision-making. The Italian elitist Pareto (1968: 27), for example, argues that 'the greater part of human actions have their origin not in logical reasoning but in sentiment'.

Even if a society were governed by elites, political decisions would still be necessary within and between elites. Also, elite decisions need to be communicated to the masses and this process is itself political in that information has to be filtered, prioritised and framed by laws. Some elitists also recognise that the history of the last few hundred years has included the struggle by ordinary people for influence over the government of their lives. The spread of democratic institutions globally is testimony to this. Therefore, some elite theories argue for what is called **democratic-elitism.**

Schumpeter (1976) is one of those who argues for the inevitability of elite rule but who nonetheless recognises that, at the very least, the masses will wish to be consulted on which elites govern them. He therefore suggests the most stable form of government would be one run by elites but who are accountable to the masses through regular elections. Of course, in totalitarian states there may be no need for elites to concede so much ground to democracy. Such states aim to rule through force and intimidation. Nonetheless, even in totalitarian states like the former Soviet Union gestures towards democracy were made. Soviet leaders referred to their country as a democracy, and elections (albeit with no choice of party) and some consultation with ordinary people did take place.

Elite rule in its purest form is then extremely hard to establish and maintain. The desire for deliberation and consultation amongst ordinary people, as well as the struggle between elites for power ensures that politics creeps back into even the most elitist and closed system of decision-making. Moreover, it is doubtful whether we can be optimistic about the capacity of elites to rule our affairs effectively. Countless examples can be found of allegedly 'superior' elites making decisions that lead to war, internal suppression of minorities, human rights abuses and economic turmoil, the two world wars of the twentieth century being the most dramatic illustrations. It could be argued, therefore, that dispersing decision-making as widely as possible represents the most effective way of saving us from the 'wisdom' of experts.

Politics as means to a greater end

History is full of examples of individuals, groups and movements who see politics as at best a temporary measure: as a means to a greater end. Politics presupposes conflict, otherwise we would have no need for it. After all, why spend time debating an issue when there is no disagreement? Some political movements, however, consciously aim to create a situation where conflict, and therefore the need for politics, disappears. Such visions are utopian in that their ultimate aim is to create a self-regulating and harmonious community of equals.

Marxism is one of those movements that has often been accused of asserting a dangerous utopianism, where political action is merely one method for pushing society towards what Marxists see as the inevitable goal of **communism**. As Callinicos (1984: 124) notes, 'Marxism . . . seeks the abolition of politics'. It is doubtful how realistic this goal is. Kolakowski (1978: 523) concludes his huge three-volume analysis of Marxism as follows: 'Marxism has been the greatest fantasy of our century. It was a dream offering the prospect of a society of perfect unity, in which all human aspirations would be fulfilled and all values reconciled.'

For Marx, politics was secondary to economics. The primary division in modern **capitalist societies** was between the owners of wealth (the bourgeoisie) and the real producers of wealth (the proletariat). Marx felt that the inevitable conflict between a wealthy few and an increasingly alienated majority would lead to the abolition of private property and the eventual creation of a communist society run on co-operative grounds. Despite the numerous interpretations of Marx's work, it is pretty clear that Marx felt the primary vehicle for this transformation would be violent revolution. The aim of such a revolution was to end the need for politics by destroying the main source of social division, namely private property. At a stroke, the two problems that give rise to politics disappear.

First, the productive capacity of industrial society would ensure there would be plentiful resources. Second, the abolition of the class system (which is rooted in the division between owners and non-owners of the means of production) would ensure that value conflicts would be a thing of the past. Marxism tends to grant democratic politics a secondary role in the struggle for the realisation of communism. Marx welcomed the extension of civil rights (such as free speech) and political rights (such as voting) to the working classes only in as far as these rights enabled the development of **class consciousness** amongst the proletariat. It was this recognition of the common interests that all working people shared that would ensure the destruction of capitalism through revolutionary action rather than political reform.

The problem with these kinds of arguments, though perhaps well intentioned in theory, is that in practice they have led to particularly brutal forms of elite rule. Revolutions claiming Marx's ideas as their inspiration, such as in Russia in 1917 or China in 1949, have invariably been led, not by the proletariat themselves, as Marx had intended, but by elites *claiming* to represent the interests of the proletariat. Where such revolutions have been 'successful', the result has been in the short term violent persecution of minorities and in the long term the suppression of the whole of society. This is, of course, a far cry from Marx's intentions. Nonetheless, his love of exalting violence and dismissal of morality as 'bourgeois illusion' did create the possibility that Marx's ideas would be used to justify the oppression of those who failed to see where their 'real' interests lay.

The illusion of a world without politics, of a harmonious unity between people, has ironically led to some of the most inhuman treatment of people imaginable. It could be argued that the idea of politics as a means to a greater end is merely an extreme version of politics as the pursuit of power. It is not the case (as Marx hoped) that politics disappears in communist society. Rather, politics becomes centred upon the will of the leader or the party, with all the oppression of dissidents or 'unbelievers' this necessarily entails. This is because any attempt to achieve a utopia of peace and order via any means necessary is a contradiction in terms and undoubtedly lends considerable weight to arguments of writers such as Crick who suggest violence is not a legitimate method of politics but its polar opposite.

SUMMARY

We have seen in this chapter that politics is an 'essentially contested' concept: it is a word and a practice that is capable of meaning many things to many people. Politics, however it is defined, is a response to certain inherent human problems, and in particular the problems of order and distribution of resources.

The idea of politics as compromise between opposed positions suggests that through such methods as diplomacy, collective decision-making, conflict resolution and deliberation, we can resolve our differences without appeal to violence. In contrast, the theory that politics is nothing more than the pursuit of power, by whatever means necessary, allows for a much broader definition of the concept. Such an approach has been useful to those, such as feminists, who wish to point to how even interpersonal relationships in our private lives can be important areas of domination and exclusion from decision-making. Including violence as a necessary part of our definition of political activity, however, runs the risks of squeezing out peaceful solutions to our problems and creating a cynical attitude towards politics generally. There is little doubt that even in long-established democracies politics is too often seen as part of the problem rather than a solution to the problems communities face. This 'crisis of politics' can be illustrated by the lack of trust citizens have in their politicians and systems of **governance**.

A cynical attitude towards politics is one of the motivating forces behind theories that advocate alternatives to politics such as the market, rule by elites, or the transcendence of politics through violent revolution. We have seen how in fact none of these alternatives can in practice deliver us from politics. The free market cannot resolve all our moral differences and by generating large-scale inequalities creates problems of its own. Leaving decisions to experts does not dispense with politics but, at most, limits its sphere of operation. Theories such as Marxism aim to transcend politics altogether but in practice no country governed by Marxist ideals has come even close to achieving this goal.

It seems impossible to realistically envisage a world without politics. Given it seeks to resolve fundamental human problems, it is imperative that we all try to understand politics better. To that end, the two remaining chapters in this section will explore in more detail some key concepts and approaches in political analysis.

FURTHER READING

Calvocoressi's (2000) impressive overview of the causes and consequences of conflict across the globe since 1945 is a powerful reminder of just why human beings need politics. A particularly stimulating collection of essays that explore the nature of politics is Leftwich (1984). Three entertaining books that take contrasting views of the scope of politics are Crick (2000), Laver (1983) and Minogue (1995). For a classic guide to power politics in practice see Machiavelli (1961). On the consequences for citizen participation of an increasing cynicism towards politics see Dalton (1996). Nozick (1974) presents a forceful case for strictly limiting the scope of politics in favour of the free market. Bottomore (1993a) presents an interesting, critical survey of elite theory. Finally, Thomas (1994) is a brave attempt to reconstruct a Marxist theory of politics in the wake of the failures of communism in practice.

2 KEY CONCEPTS IN POLITICAL ANALYSIS

In the previous chapter we saw how diverse definitions of politics can be. According to some perspectives, politics would appear to encompass *all* human relationships. Laver provides a good example of a broad definition in the opening lines of his 1983 book *Invitation to Politics*:

> Politics is about groups of people. It is about the interplay of hopes and fears, aims and aspirations, that can be found in any group . . . politics is about the characteristic blend of conflict and co-operation that can be found so often in human interactions. Pure conflict is war. Pure co-operation is true love. Politics is a mixture of both. I will go further, and claim that *any* mixture of conflict and co-operation is politics. (Laver 1983: 1)

For the student of Politics this is not particularly helpful. For as Leftwich (1984: 120) comments, the dangers of such a broad approach are that 'the subject-matter loses any clear focus, and the discipline of politics becomes substantively and methodologically undisciplined, merging with everything else'. Because of this problem, as well as for some even more convincing reasons that will become evident in this and the next chapter, political scientists have tended to focus on particular aspects of human interactions.

Political scientists have been concerned above all with how societies are governed. The discipline of Politics is then focused upon the question of *governance*, where governance is defined as: *the resolution of the problems of order and the distribution of material and cultural resources at a societal level through the making and enforcing of binding rules.* This core focus leads the political scientist logically to investigate such related questions as:

1. How are the rules that govern societies made?
2. Who makes these rules?
3. Do these rules serve the interests of the whole of the community or just part of it?
4. How are these rules enforced and by what institutions?

In order to systematically address these questions, political scientists employ a number of concepts. A concept is an abstract, general idea that we use to make sense of the world around us. Concepts allow us to classify and explain human behaviour and are an essential tool if we are to begin to find answers to the questions listed above. Political scientists have developed a multitude of such concepts and have borrowed a good few more from other disciplines. However, of all the concepts employed in the study of politics, the vast majority of political scientists would agree that the ideas of **power** and the **state** are central to the discipline.

Because of their importance to the study of politics, this chapter will focus upon the concepts of power and the state in some detail. In exploring each, I will look at how they have commonly been defined and what the main controversies are that surround them. The final section of the chapter will be concerned with the challenge the concept of **globalisation** presents to political science. Political scientists have tended to focus much of their attention on the governance of particular societies, often studying them in isolation from other societies. Globalisation suggests that this focus is no longer legitimate, as technological advances have lead to the breakdown of clear boundaries between societies, perhaps even heralding the beginning of the end of the state. We shall see, however, that the state, as the primary focal point of power in the world, is still far from irrelevant as a crucial area of study in political science.

POLITICAL SCIENCE AND POWER

Leftwich (1984: 10) usefully observes how conceptions of politics can be divided into two kinds:

It is fair to say that the single most important factor involved in influencing the way people implicitly or explicitly perceive of politics is whether they define it primarily in terms of *process*, or whether they define it in terms of the place or places where it happens, that is in terms of an *arena*, or institutional forum.

For those who perceive politics to be essentially a process where decisions, influence and resources flow from one group to another, power is perhaps the key concept of political analysis. An example of this can be found in Harold Lasswell's (1936) classic study of the distribution of power in which he focuses upon the question of 'who gets what, when, how'.

What Lasswell was seeking to discover in his study was which individuals and groups were able to most successfully exercise their will, achieve their goals and resist opposition from those opposed to the achievement of their objectives. This is in essence what we mean by power in a political context. The German social scientist Max Weber defines power more eloquently. Power is, for Weber (1948: 180), 'The chance of a man or a number of men to realise their own will in a communal action even against the resistance of others who are participating in the action'. In a political context power is not just having the capacity to carry out an action (which is roughly how standard dictionaries would define the term); it is the ability to act successfully even in the face of opposition. Despite the apparent simplicity of Weber's definition, the study of power is anything but straightforward. A good way to begin analysing the controversies surrounding power is to look at a particularly important intervention into the debate by the radical social thinker Stephen Lukes.

In his short book *Power: A Radical View*, Lukes (1974) criticises what he sees as the naïve approach to power adopted by many postwar political scientists. According to **pluralists** like Lasswell it was the job of the political scientist to identify the outcomes of decisions by measuring which social actors benefited in terms of the accumulation of more resources or greater influence over others within a community. Another influential pluralist, Robert Dahl (1957: 201), argued that power was exercised (and could therefore be measured) when actor A succeeded in getting actor B 'to do something that B would not otherwise do'. For the pluralists of the 1950s and 1960s, then, power entailed the making and enforcing of decisions at the collective level. The political scientist interested in the exercise of power might study the outcomes of decisions in parliament, for example, in order to explain which social groups benefit from particular acts of parliament. It might be, for instance, that a campaign by the **Trade Union Congress** (TUC), in the face of vocal opposition from employers, leads to the passing of legislation which extends workers' **rights.** In this case, it would be fair to say that the TUC has exercised a degree of power, all be it indirectly, by influencing the passing of legislation by the government.

Pluralists who focus only upon the empirically observable outcomes of decision-making are, argues Lukes, missing the point. Lukes accepts that the outcomes of decisions are an important aspect of power but are only part of the story. Lukes was also interested in the context in which decisions were made. He suggests that we should understand the exercise of power, not just in the one-dimensional sense of decision-making, but as a three-dimensional process.

As well as decision-making, it is important to look at *non-decision*-making. For Lukes, the most powerful social actors, such as governments, have the capacity not only to make decisions which further their interests but also to prevent decisions, or even discussion, on some issues. This is what we mean when we talk about controlling the **political agenda:** some opinions on what should be done about a particular issue may well be marginalised or excluded completely from access to decision-making processes. British socialists, for example, have often complained that because all the major political parties broadly support the free market as their favoured approach to economic management the alternatives, such as state planning or publicly funded workers' co-operatives, are never seriously discussed or considered as policy options.

One of the attractions of the classical pluralist model of power was that it was relatively easy to measure. Decisions could be observed and outcomes of those decisions identified. By introducing the idea of non-decision-making we considerably complicate the concept of power. Are some issues and opinions *deliberately* excluded from the political agenda? This is of course a very hard question to answer and almost certainly impossible to prove conclusively through the gathering of evidence. If our political elites are conspiring together to marginalise particular social interests they are not likely to admit it to an inquisitive political scientist! Nonetheless, political scientists can gain some insight into non-decision-making by exploring the extent to which citizens are content with their political institutions. High levels of alienation from their systems of governance may well indicate that some groups of citizens do not believe politicians are truly representing their interests.

Lukes further complicates things by introducing a third dimension in his discussion of power. He argues that even if citizens do appear content with their lot this may in fact reflect the ability elites have to manipulate the desires and feelings of ordinary people. We might learn to accept or even celebrate a humble social position, oblivious to the fact that our real interests are being ignored or even undermined. This third dimension of power raises a very important methodological question in the social sciences generally. To what extent can any individual exercise their will, without the objectives they pursue being influenced or even determined by the social context in which they act? Lukes' theory suggests that even our most strongly held beliefs about what is in our own interest might well be the product of what Marxists refer to as **false consciousness.** There are real problems with Lukes' third dimension of power, however. The main difficulty is who is to say what someone else's *real* interests might be. By denying that actors know their own interests and attributing their motivations and actions to a false consciousness is to make a value judgement that cannot be proved right one way or the other.

Having looked at some of the controversies surrounding the concept, we shall move on to examine how power might be classified. What questions should we ask when we are trying to identify and explain the use and abuse of power?

Classifying power

In analysing and seeking to explain political behaviour and the practice of governance, political scientists, implicitly or explicitly, will make assumptions about the nature of power. Although not all political scientists will agree with the various ways in which power is characterised below, consciously addressing the following six questions is a useful starting point for the analysis of any particular act of power.

1. *What type of power is being used?*
In modern societies, a number of different types of power can be observed. The three most important are military, communicative and economic.

Military power is the use of organised force. It is primarily deployed by states, either to maintain social order at home or to protect a state's interests abroad. Its use can be most obviously observed when states go to **war.** Military power can also be used by non-state oganisations, such as terrorist groups, who seek to influence, overthrow or destroy a particular government. Communicative power refers to the control of ideas. This form of power might be utilised by a charismatic political leader, Adolf Hitler for example, who seeks to influence the beliefs and actions of others through persuasion, manipulation and propaganda. Economic power involves the control of wealth and the means to produce that wealth. Private companies, wealthy individuals and the state (with its tax-raising powers and direct involvement in economic activity through state-owned industries and services) possess this form of power.

Since political elites will tend to utilise all three kinds of power, it is useful to understand political power as encompassing them all. As Mann (1986: 27) observes, 'Political power is necessarily centralised and territorial, and in these respects differs from the other power sources'. In the modern world, this centralisation that Mann refers to has been undertaken by the state. It is the state, as a unique human institution, that has had the capacity to most successfully centralise and utilise the forms of power discussed above. Because the state is the most powerful institution and the dominant form of governance in the modern world, political science has focused its attention upon it.

2. Where is it being exercised?

This question is concerned with the location or arena of power. Some social scientists, particularly sociologists, have analysed the exercise of power within the family or other small social groups and institutions. Political scientists, for the reasons set out above, have tended to focus their attention upon the state.

3. What resources are being deployed?

To successfully exercise power any social actor will require access to resources. These might include wealth, military arms, technology, reputation, charisma and information.

4. What methods are being utilised?

Those actors seeking to achieve their objectives draw upon a number of methods. These range from physical force to peaceful persuasion. In order to achieve stable governance, political elites will tend to try to avoid the use of force whenever possible because of the costs and risks involved and will instead seek to legitimise their power by attempting to convert it into authority. **Authority** is perhaps the most secure form of power because it entails the recognition by those who are ruled that their leaders have the *right* to rule. Authority can usefully be defined then as legitimate power, involving as it does some degree of consent on the part of the ruled.

5. *What is the social context?*

All acts of power occur within a social context. The term *social structures* is used by social scientists generally to refer to the background against which decisions are taken and rules are made. These structures refer to physical, social and cultural attributes that define individuals and social groups. Examples would be gender, 'race', and class. A crucial issue for political scientists is the extent to which these structures shape or even determine the exercise of power. Some feminists, for example, would insist that power is exercised in the context of a system of **patriarchy** where the institutions and values of politics are overwhelmingly defined and controlled by men. It is always the case then that when a social actor exercises power they do not do so in circumstances of their own choosing and that these circumstances will tend to favour one interest over another.

6. *What are the outcomes?*

Political scientists are also interested in the results that ensue from the use of power. This takes us back to Lasswell's famous question: who gets what, when, how? Political scientists aim to measure the material, cultural and psychological conse-quences of the use of power. The outcomes of any particular act of power are a useful indicator of the likely future power relationships between particular social groups.

POLITICAL SCIENCE AND THE STATE

As we have seen, political science has tended to focus its attention upon the question of governance: how is power institutionalised into systems of decision-making? Because the state is the primary form of governance found in the modern world, contemporary political scientists have devoted a great deal of their time to studying it. No other institution in the world is able to so successfully concentrate military, communicative and economic power.

Max Weber once again provides us with a useful starting point for the analysis of this concept. For Weber (1948: 78), the state can be defined as 'a human community that successfully claims the monopoly of the legitimate use of physical force within a given territory'. Like his definition of power discussed earlier, Weber's apparently straightforward definition masks a number of complexities and contradictions that have exercised the minds of students of politics. Weber, like many political scientists since, thought that the key defining characteristic of the state was its ultimate reliance upon force. This element of Weber's perspective on the state, however, clearly does not sit well with the other elements of his definition: monopoly, **legitimacy** and territory. The very existence of the state presupposes that there are some individuals and groups who actively resist its claim to a monopoly of force: if the state truly enjoyed a monopoly of arms, there would be no need for the state! The concept of legitimate force is also problematic because it is highly questionable whether physical force can ever be legitimate in the eyes of its victim, and in this sense force and legitimacy are mutually exclusive methods of power. Finally, the fact that even the most powerful states rule over only a limited geographical area means that they are faced with potent rivals in the form of other states and therefore can never be completely secure: one state's security is another's insecurity!

In the context of a world dominated by states, the idea of politics as peaceful compromise between opposing views always lives in the shadow of the threat of violence. Some scholars have a made a virtue of this by reducing politics to the threat or use of force. Nicholson (1984: 39), for example, argues that 'even where force is not used, it could be: its possible exercise is always there, and that is what is distinctive about politics'. Other commentators have argued that the use of violence obliterates politics all together (Crick, 2000). It is partly the tension between these kinds of theoretical positions that has made the state such a controversial concept in political thought: does the state facilitate or thwart politics?

Questions surrounding the nature and desirability of a world governed by states have helped structure much political analysis: What would the world be like without a state? Why should I obey the state? What can the state do for me and what should I do for it? Some theorists, such as Hegel, celebrate the modern state as the highest possible form of human community because it is based upon rational and legal principles, such as the **rule of law,** and therefore provides a sound background against which humanity can develop its intellectual and cultural potential. In contrast, anarchists like Proudhon have seen the state as the main oppressor of human freedom and have made the destruction of the state their primary goal.

It is important to remember that although for good reason the state has provided the main institutional focus for contemporary political science (whether in an attempt to understand, celebrate or transcend it), it is not the only institution that has been concerned with the collective rule-making associated with human governance. The state is not only a philosophical idea; it is a historical entity, and a fairly recent one at that. The first embryonic states, sometimes referred to as pristine states, appeared in Mesopotamia around 3000 BC. For most of human history then communities survived and often flourished without a state. In stateless communities, rules were generally obeyed because of close kinship ties, custom and persuasion rather than the threat or use of force. The state is then just one possible attempt to resolve the problem of order and the distribution of resources. Why, then, has it become the dominant form of governance in the modern world?

One of the most systematic and convincing theories of the origins of the state has been developed by the political sociologist Michael Mann (1993). Mann has coined the useful phrase 'social caging' to refer to the process whereby the boundaries of the state gradually became more clearly defined over time. For Mann, the first states appeared in order to co-ordinate the production, management and protection of the resources required for large-scale agricultural production in response to population growth. The coordination of mass production created a need for political and military elites, who in turn sought to centralise power still further into ever more sophisticated and powerful institutions of governance. Consequently, those individuals who found themselves within the confines of the state's jurisdiction were increasingly locked into a compulsory relationship with governments.

Once the institution of the state became established, its advantages became apparent. States were more easily able to organise themselves economically and militarily and so as Harris (1993: 313) notes, 'once states come into existence, they tend to spread, engulf, and overwhelm non-state peoples'. As Giddens (1985) has highlighted in his study of the development of the modern state, technology played a crucial role in allowing elites to centralise power. Before the advent of the modern state, the technologies of surveillance and communication did not exist to allow elites to successfully cage their populations into a permanent power relationship. In the Feudal age, for example, widespread illiteracy, the lack of a mass system of communication and the inadequacy of the transport system meant that power was inevitably fragmented. This is why Giddens argues that pre-modern states had frontiers rather than borders: rulers simply did not have the resources of power necessary to guarantee their borders.

With the technological innovations in printing techniques, railways and telegraph communications associated with the industrial revolution (which began in Britain in the eighteenth century), the task of centralising power became increasingly more plausible. Mann (1993: 25) continues his metaphor of the social cage by claiming that as state boundaries became firmer, so individuals became increasingly subject to surveillance by 'two principal zookeepers: tax gatherers and recruiting officers'. For Mann, however, the strengthening of the bars on the cage of the state was not all bad for the individual citizen. Once individuals could no longer escape being locked into a permanent relationship with the state, the desire to make conditions inside the cage more palatable increased. The gradual growth in the power of representative parliaments, the extension of the franchise to workers and women and the development of the **welfare state** can all interpreted as the product of struggle for greater control *over* the state, through the extension of political rights, and claims to greater entitlements *from* the state in the form of publicly funded **social rights.**

Today the modern state, and especially Western states, has concentrated unprecedented degrees of power in all its forms. In terms of military power, further advances in technology have meant that the armed forces of states possess extraordinary destructive capacity. Information technology has also meant that states have highly sophisticated instruments through which to utilise communicative power, and the rise of the spin doctor is one fairly trivial example of how political elites are consciously making ever greater use of the power of the media to present their policies in the best possible light. The state's economic power is also very significant. In many modern states, between one third and one half of gross domestic product is collected as taxes to be used as the government sees fit (Ball and Peters 2000: 4). However, as shall be discussed below, according to some theories of globalisation the state's capacity for exercising power may be diminishing. Before critically assessing this contention, let us conclude with a summary of the main characteristics found in the modern state.

Classifying the state

Sovereignty
This concept refers to the state's claim to be the most powerful institution within a given territory. The state is unique amongst human institutions because it demands both universal and compulsory jurisdiction within its borders. Whatever an individual's particular view of the state might be, if they reside within its borders they are subject to its laws. Other human communities, such as private clubs, trade unions, or

political parties, allow the individual to revoke their membership if they so choose. In contrast, it is extremely difficult to escape the power of the state. In a world made up of states, leaving behind the laws of one via emigration will inevitably mean placing oneself under the jurisdiction of another.

Rational and legal rule

The modern state rests its authority partly upon its claim to govern through the making and enforcing of rational laws. Weber contrasts this modernist idea of the **rule of law,** which does not base its authority upon the personal attributes of rulers, with more arbitrary and emotive forms of governance that derive their power either from the charisma of individual leaders or from tradition and custom. Many modern states seek to ensure that the rule of law is upheld through the instrument of an independent judiciary that is in theory separate from the legislative and executive functions of the state (see Chapter 5).

Military power

As Weber's definition discussed above highlights, the state's claim to authority rests ultimately upon its concentration of military power. If the state is threatened by either its own citizens or by other states it can seek to protect its existence through the use of violence. An irony at the heart of modern politics is then that on one hand the state claims to provide a peaceful framework for individuals to live their lives, while on the other hand citizens have often found that the greatest threat to their basic rights has been their own state.

Citizenship

Despite their capacity for violence, states will, as a rule, avoid the use of force whenever possible: the use of force is costly and its results uncertain. Partly for this reason, and partly because citizens themselves have struggled for it, many modern states have operated on the basis that their populations are citizens who enjoy rights rather than subjects who are at the mercy of the arbitrary rule of their leaders. Modern states

derive much of their authority then from their claim to protect
citizens' civil and political freedoms. The historical and ongoing extension of democratic mechanisms of government
across the globe can in part be explained by the desire of
states to legitimise their power in the eyes of their citizens.

Imagined communities
Although Weber defines the state as a human community in
fact it is more accurate to describe the institution as an
association. Following the work of the German sociologist
Ferdinand Tonnies, a community implies bonds of affection
between its members whereas the idea of an association
implies a much looser and perhaps more instrumental affilia-
tion between individuals. Because of the need to ensure loyalty
and obedience their its laws, states have attempted to bridge
the gap between community and association by consciously
promoting what Anderson (1983) has called 'imagined communities'. The most obvious example of this is the encourage-
ment of national sentiment through such methods as public
education and the creation of national symbols such as flags,
heroes and myths. This is why when we talk about the modern
state we tend to add the term nation to form the term *nation-
state*. The state claims to represent the interests of a particular
nation although in practice no states enjoy the kind of cultural
homogeneity that the term nation-state implies. In practice,
states are multinational and multicultural in character.

THE CHALLENGE OF GLOBALISATION

Definitions of globalisation are legion, but in simple terms
globalisation can be understood as *the growing interdependence of peoples, cultures and economies*. By itself, this
definition does not imply that states are no longer powerful
and influential actors. Some moderate theorists of globalisation such as Dicken (1998: 7) have accepted that 'nation-states
continue to be key players' but contend that states now govern
in a rapidly changing context that is more internationalised

than ever before. For Dicken, states are finding it harder to exert control over their economies and citizens because communication and commerce across national boundaries is more extensive and intensive than ever before. Radical versions of the globalisation thesis, as advanced for example by Ohmae (1995), go much further than this, however. They claim that globalisation is leading to the end of the nation-state. Given these claims, political scientists, who have made the state their primary focus of study, have strong reasons for studying theories of globalisation.

There are three main elements to the radical globalisation thesis. First is the claim that cultural differences between nations are diminishing in the face of the development of a global consumerist culture. Second, large private companies, often called **transnational corporations** (TNCs), are 'footloose' actors that can transcend geography by moving their production and services from region to region in search of lower taxes, cheaper labour and more favourable employment legislation. Third, the world economy is effectively borderless as investment and consumer activities stretch across the globe. It is the rapid advance in technology in the last few decades, and in particular information and travel technologies, that has been the main facilitator of each of these three aspects of globalisation.

There can be little doubt that globalisation is not a complete fantasy. One only has to observe the spread of instantly recognisable brand names such as Coca-Cola or McDonald's, the huge growth in the wealth of firms like General Motors, and the instantaneous exchange of billions of pounds on the world's stock markets to see that technological innovations have intensified long-standing processes of internationalisation. Many political scientists therefore accept that moderate theories of globalisation have a point. However, it is very doubtful whether globalisation in its more extreme form is accurate in its claim that we are witnessing the 'end of the nation-state'. There is good reason to suspect that Ohmae's thesis greatly exaggerates the effects of globalisation.

Firstly, there is no reason to suppose that technological

advances necessarily mean that cultures will become fused into one universal culture. Drinking the same soft drink or eating the same kind of burger is one thing, but deeper and more fundamental identities (such as nationality) are much harder to change. There is ample evidence of diversity in religion, **ideology** and social practices to refute the idea of cultural globalisation. As dramatically illustrated by the destruction of the World Trade Center in the USA in September 2001, these differences can still lead to considerable conflict between cultures that has to be managed politically. In fact, technology has helped diverse cultures conserve their values through access to relatively cheap forms of communication such as the internet, CDs and videos. Communication technology has in many cases accented rather than diminished cultural differences. The destructive capacity of modern weapons technology makes the consequences of differences descending into conflict even more frightening.

Secondly, the notion that TNCs are footloose and operate outside of the regulatory framework of states is also dubious. The vast majority of TNCs have most of their assets concentrated in and are managed by nationals in their home state. Many countries, such as Japan and Germany for example, do not experience the kind of levels of internal investment by foreign companies that would be expected in a truly global economy. Moreover, states still provide the regulatory framework and much of the infrastructure (such as education, training and transport networks) that are the essential context for markets to operate effectively.

Thirdly, although world trade has intensified in the last few decades it is still heavily concentrated in particular regions, with the European Union, Japan and USA very much dominant. Some regions, particularly parts of Africa and Latin America, have such a small share of world trade that perhaps a more accurate description of world trade patterns is *polarisation* rather than globalisation. The dominance by Western states of those organisations that do exist to give some regulation to the world economy, such as the **World Bank** or **World Trade Organisation,** lends considerable weight to the argument that economic globalisation is little more than the assertion of the interests of the most powerful states such as the USA and Britain. In this respect, it could be argued that states still matter, it's just that some matter more than others.

Perhaps the most pervasive aspect of globalisation is the growing realisation that many of the problems states face have a global dimension to them and cannot be managed success-fully by a single state acting alone. Such 'global risks' as ecological disasters, the threat of nuclear or biological conflict, international crime, enforced migration, and world poverty are no respecters of state borders and require greater inter-national co-operation if they are to begin to be solved. It is difficult to imagine how these problems can be addressed by the free market alone, as Ohmae implies they can.

There is some evidence to suggest that states are beginning to realise that their own interests can no longer be easily separated from those of other states. We can see the beginning of an **international society** as witnessed by the development of global organisations such as the United Nations and the coming together of states into regional bodies such the Eur-opean Union. The authority of many such collective organisa-tions is far from established and stable, however, and what power they do possess is derived directly from their member states. What is clear then is that whatever the nature of future governance might be, at present states remain by far the most powerful actors globally and domestically and therefore re-main a legitimate focus of study for political science.

SUMMARY

Political scientists are particularly interested in how societies are governed and the nature of the rules that bind individuals to the collective will of the community. In order to system-atically explore this question of governance, the concepts of power and the state have proved extremely useful.

Power can be understood as the successful exercise of the will of one social actor over that of another. Some commentators have argued, however, that such a simple view of power is one-dimensional. To really understand who gets what, when and how it is also important to explore the context in which decision-making takes place. Radicals like Lukes have contended that the most powerful political actors are not just able to make decisions that favour their own interests. They can also exclude opposing interests by controlling the content of the political agenda and can deceive many of those excluded from decision-making into believing that it is their interests (not those of elites) that are being served. Because of the problems of measuring such elusive ideas as manipulation, not all political scientists have accepted Lukes' theory. Despite a lack of agreement on the exact nature of power, questions such as what resources, methods and outcomes are involved in the making and enforcement of collective rules remain crucial to the study of politics.

The state, as the primary form of governance in the modern world, is no less controversial. Weber's definition of the state as an institution that claims a monopoly of legitimate force in a particular territory highlights a number of deep tensions at the heart of modern systems of politics. How can an institution that bases its rule on force be truly legitimate? By dividing the world into competitive states, do we not risk destroying rather than ensuring order? Such questions continue to exercise the minds of political scientists because the state is simply too powerful an institution to ignore if we wish to explain and perhaps even improve our systems of governance.

This last point remains true even in the face of theories of globalisation that suggest the state is fast becoming redundant because of a growing interdependence of peoples, cultures and economies driven primarily by technological innovation. Many of the assertions made by radical versions of the globalisation thesis are, however, unproven. Diversity rather than uniformity best describes cultural practices; growing inequality rather than global affluence characterises the present state of the world economy. This diversity and inequality are rooted in a states system that remains as significant as ever to human governance, given the lack of alternative and effective forms of rule. It may well be that the problems associated with global risks, such as ecological meltdown for example, can only be managed by new forms of governance that are themselves global in nature. For political scientists who seek to understand how power and rule are institutionalised and exercised, however, it seems inevitable that for the foreseeable future the state will remain a crucial focal point of analysis.

FURTHER READING

Dahl's (1961) now classic pluralist study of power in an American city is still well worth reading. Lukes' (1974) extended essay on power provides a very accessible critique of such pluralist approaches, while in turn Hay's (1997) short article usefully highlights some of the weaknesses in Lukes' own theory. Clegg (1989) is a more extensive survey of various influential theories of power. Hoffman (1995) is an excellent introduction to the contradictions that lie at the heart of the state. Giddens (1985) and Mann (1993) provide a great deal of detail on the historical development of the modern form of the state. For a critical review of the concept of globalisation, see Faulks (1999: Chapter 3). Much more extensive analyses of recent global change can be found in Waters (1995) and Albrow (1996).

3 POLITICS AS AN ACADEMIC SUBJECT

As with all academic subjects, political science has over the years built up a canon of classic texts that are still studied closely today. It is very likely that if you are studying Politics formally you will at some stage find yourself grappling with works such as Marx and Engels' *Communist Manifesto*, Plato's *Republic*, Locke's *Two Treatises of Government*, and Machiavelli's *The Prince*. Many of the great thinkers whose ideas are taught within the modern political science curriculum would not, however, have described themselves purely (if at all) as political scientists. Marx, for example, was a historian, an economist, a philosopher, a sociologist and amateur mathematician, as well as a political theorist and activist! What these great thinkers have in common is their holistic approach to the great concerns of their day. Questions of politics, society, economics and indeed ethics were seen as closely interrelated and needed to be studied together, drawing upon a wide range of approaches, methods and concepts in order to comprehend them.

Today we are more used to knowledge being organised into discrete subject areas and so in the final chapter of this section I look in more detail at how Politics is defined as an academic discipline. The chapter is divided into two main parts. First, I outline some important developments in the history of political science. Second, I examine whether Politics can be scientific, exploring in this context the role values play in political enquiry.

THE DEVELOPMENT OF POLITICAL SCIENCE

It was in the eighteenth century that philosophers such as Hegel first began to make clear distinctions between the **state** (the political), **civil society** (the social) and the family (the private) and thereby created the conceptual space for the development of distinctive branches of social science. As Bottomore comments (1993: 2), political science 'owes its characteristic development since the eighteenth century to the establishment of a clear distinction between the "political" and the social, the constitution of "society" as an object of systematic enquiry, and the consequent reflection upon the relations between political and social life'. The break-up of the study of human behaviour into discrete academic disciplines was further advanced by developments in economic theory. In the nineteenth century, economics began to emerge as a specialist academic subject which had until then been intimately connected with the analysis of politics and usually went under the name **political economy.** Scholars such as Menger and Jevons argued that economics should instead be considered as the *science of rational action within the economic market place* and as such could be studied in isolation from political forces. With the rise of the modern university in the second half of the nineteenth century, and in keeping with the general division of labour that the industrial revolution heralded, fields of knowledge were increasingly pigeon-holed into particular academic subjects. The social sciences did not escape this development and the social, political and economic aspects of human life began to be studied separately by professional sociologists, political scientists and economists.

It is fair to say that of the three main social sciences, Politics has been the most unreflective in defining itself as a discrete subject area and it remains today a highly eclectic discipline. As Stoker (1995: 1) notes, political scientists have mostly been content 'just do it rather than talk about it'. This has meant that the subject has developed in rather an *ad hoc* way and has left Politics vulnerable to the charge that it is not really a subject at all. Sociologists, for example, have sometimes argued that as politics cannot in practice be separated from wider social forces it should be studied as one aspect of their much broader discipline (Rush 1992: 4–5).

Nevertheless, up to the Second World War political scientists themselves were pretty clear what their subject matter was. Graeme Moodie, a former Professor of Politics at York University, was a politics student in the 1940s. He describes how at that time: 'Politics was remarkably unselfconscious . . . [it] was centred upon the state and no further argument was required.' (Moodie 1984: 20) As Moodie explains, the Politics curriculum was dominated by this institutional focus upon the state on the one hand and the reading of the great classics of political thought on the other. The study of political institutions and the history of political ideas are still at the heart of the subject of Politics. In the postwar period, however, these traditional topics have been augmented by a number of alternative approaches that each sought to dramatically shift the focus of the subject. Three particularly significant challenges have been behaviouralism, **Marxism** and **feminism**.

Behaviouralism

Behaviouralism first emerged as an approach to the study of psychology and grew in influence amongst political scientists from the 1940s onwards. The aim of this movement was to move the focus of political analysis away from its traditional concern with the state and classical texts and towards the systematic analysis of political behaviour. As Blondel (1981: 25) observes, for the first time 'mass politics [became] a major subject of enquiry'. Political scientists began to focus their attention upon the study of elections, pressure groups and social movements.

For the behaviouralists, political science had for too long been unsystematic in its **methodology**. Behaviouralism was particularly sceptical about the value of **normative theory**, which they saw as the assertion of how things should be rather than an analysis of how things actually are. The role of theory should instead be a more limited one; to set out hypotheses that could then be tested through empirical study. Behaviouralists championed what they saw as more rigorous, scientific methods of surveys and statistical analyses in order to understand political phenomena. It was asserted that valid conclusions about political action could only be made if they were founded upon the objective analysis of empirical data, such as election results. It was in this new 'scientific' context that David Easton could announce the end of political theory as it had once been, and Peter Laslett could declare that 'for the moment, anyway, political philosophy is dead' (Ball 1995: 40–41).

Behaviouralism has been criticised, however, for failing to see the wood for the trees. Sanders (1995), for example, identifies behaviouralism's tendency towards mindless empiricism: lots of statistics are generated about relatively unimportant issues and the big questions of politics, such as how we can resolve deep conflicts between diverse interests, are left unanswered. This is why normative political theory has stubbornly refused to die. Moreover, it is also doubtful whether the behaviouralists themselves were as objective in their work as they claimed (see below).

Despite these criticisms, behaviouralism has served at least two useful purposes for political science. First, behaviouralism has helped force political scientists to take questions of methodology seriously and be more explicit about the tools of analysis they are employing. Second, by focusing upon the political activities of ordinary people as they vote, protest or lobby, behaviouralists have helped broaden out the study of political action in ways that have undoubtedly enhanced our understanding of how politics operates in practice.

Marxism

Marxism first emerged as a influential approach to political science in British universities in the 1960s. Marxism has a rather different relationship to Politics than other rival 'approaches' because it offers such a distinctive perspective on society in general. For this reason, Marsh and Stoker (1995), in their edited book *Theory and Methods in Political Science*, consciously do not include Marxism as one of the core approaches to political science. They justify this omission by arguing that Marxism critically challenges the idea that political phenomena can be studied in isolation from other social and, in particular, economic processes. For Marxists, **the mode of production** and the relationships between social classes do, in the last analysis, shape the nature of politics and political institutions. The economic system is the base upon which all other human institutions are built and politics therefore has to be studied in that context. Marxists have therefore tended to deny the existence of an academic discipline of Politics. The very existence of such a discipline may itself be interpreted by Marxists as either the product of **false consciousness** or alternatively the result of a deliberate bourgeois trick to fool people into thinking politics has an autonomous identity that can be understood without reference to the economic system.

It is ironic then (especially given the Marxist contention that under **communism** the state would 'whither away') that for many influential Marxists such as Miliband, Poulantzas and Jessop, the main theme of Marxist political analysis since the 1960s has been Politics' traditional point of focus, namely the state. In fact, in reaction to the behaviouralists' conscious avoidance of the institution, Marxists were at the forefront of a movement in political science to 'bring the state back in' as a core issue. For behaviouralists like Easton the state was contaminated by its associations with normative political theory and was therefore 'clouded in conceptual ambiguity' (cited in Hoffman, 1995: 26). It was clear, however, that in practice the state had been growing massively in its functions and powers, in both capitalist *and* communist countries, and therefore required concentrated study by political scientists.

Marxists, driven as they are by the belief that 'politics is about the state, because the ultimate guarantee of a particular class's domination lies in its monopoly of force' undoubtedly helped political science to focus more closely upon the underlying tensions inherent in the concept of the state (Callinicos 1984: 132). The Marxist approach to state theory, although at times confused and poorly expressed, presented a very different perspective to that of non-Marxian political science. Many political scientists had tended to take the state as given, and assume that it was a logically coherent institution which acted in ways that neutrally mediated between the interests of the various groups that make up modern pluralist societies. Marxists challenged political science to explore in more detail the relationships between the state and institutions of civil society. By arguing that the state both reflected and sustained the fundamental contradictions of modern **capitalist societies**, Marxists forced political scientists to adopt a more critical approach to the state. This led to a much greater level of sophistication being employed in discussions of the state and the distribution of power and resources generally. Thus, in reaction to Marxism, mainstream political scientists such as Robert Dahl (1982) have been forced to concede that the state's apparent neutrality can often mask the considerable inequalities of **power** that exist between social classes. Powerful private companies may not directly control the state, but their huge economic leverage ensures them considerable influence over it.

Despite the claim made in some quarters that the collapse of communism in Europe since 1989 means Marxism has no longer anything of value to contribute to Politics, the ideas of Marx and his followers still provide fertile ground to the student of political science. Perhaps most importantly, Marxists have reminded us that studying the problem of **governance** without reference to how social structures such as class influence and shape political institutions is bound to be a superficial exercise.

Feminism

Feminists, who have gained some influence in the discipline since the 1970s, have, like Marxists, urged political scientists to take the impact social structures have upon politics more seriously. Instead of class, however, feminists have stressed gender relationships. Political science (as with political activity generally) has been a male-dominated profession and so the most obvious challenge feminism has made is the need to increase the number of women who are studying and indeed practising politics.

More fundamentally, feminists have shown how the institutions and concepts associated with politics are controlled and defined by men. Feminist political theorists have demonstrated how many of the 'great' texts of politics either ignore the role of women altogether or assume women are simply not political animals. It has often been argued by male theorists that women's biological make-up, or what is considered to be women's natural role as reproducers and carers, means women are creatures of emotion rather than reason. Pateman (1988) for instance shows how John Locke's theory of the **social contract** (which he argued should be the basis for our obedience to the state) is founded upon a pre-existing contract between men, which fixes women into a subordinate position. Locke (1988: 323) describes man as the 'master of a family', his subordinates including his 'wife, children, servants and slaves'. In an excellent exploration of women's negative portrayal in traditional political thought, Coole (1993) shows how assumptions about the irrationality and inferiority of women run through almost the entire canon of political theory. In terms of government, feminists have argued that the effects of policy-making upon women have been largely ignored by political science. Policies such as the creation of the **welfare state** in Britain have been premised upon the notion that men are actors in the public realm (in political and economic life) while women are primarily concerned with matters in the private realm, such as family life and household management.

It is for these reasons that feminists have urged political scientists to accept that the 'personal is political' and to rethink their analyses of politics in ways which give due weight to the experiences of women. Questions such as the distribution of resources or the use and abuse of power by men concern not only women's public lives; they are crucial in their private lives as well. Feminists have therefore pointed to how definitions of politics which ignore power relationships in the private sphere effectively exclude women's interests from the **political agenda.** A good example of how in practical terms feminists have begun to redefine the barriers between public and private is the question of domestic violence. It was common in the past for the law enforcement agencies of the state to ignore the use of violence in the home, labelling it as a 'domestic issue' and therefore not within their remit. Men's right to abuse women was in some cases enshrined in law; in the recent past married men in Britain could not be convicted of raping their wives. It is large measure due to the efforts of feminists to make domestic violence a salient political issue that has led to police forces around the country setting up specialised rape units and government passing legislation in the 1990s that has finally outlawed marital rape in Britain.

Feminists have then contributed much to redefining the political and effecting political reform. In terms of the discipline of Politics, the growth in courses in university exploring feminist political theory or the role of women in domestic and global politics is an encouraging sign that gender relations are being taken more seriously. Many mainstream political scientists, however, still ignore or pay lip service to the gender dimension of politics. There is therefore a long way to go before feminist perspectives are fully integrated into the Politics curriculum.

POLITICAL SCIENCE TODAY

In recent years, political scientists have had cause to reflect more than ever before upon the nature of their subject. This is partly in response to challenges to traditional approaches to political study, three of which were outlined above. There are, however, at least two other more practical reasons why professional political scientists in the UK are becoming more self-conscious about their discipline. Firstly, government has become increasingly concerned with issues of quality within education generally. It has therefore sought to make schools and universities more accountable by increasing the regulation of their activities through the systematic monitoring of their teaching, assessment and research. Secondly, some universities have found that demand for Politics courses has been falling and some fear, with considerable justification, that this reflects a wider disengagement with politics within society. This means that political scientists have a vested interest in presenting their subject in the most interesting and coherent way possible!

To what extent then has this self-reflection led to the identification of a core curriculum in political science? Certainly, many political thinkers remain unsure of the precise remit of the subject. Ball and Peters (2000: 19) argue that political science today is in 'a rather confused state', while Roger Scruton (1996: 423) wonders whether it is 'too wide and too ambitious to be an independent subject with a method of its own . . . [it] remains influential only as a projected unity rather than as an actual one'. In recent times the Quality Assurance Agency (QAA), which is the main government agency concerned with standards in British Universities, has been trying to encourage a more systematic approach to this question. To this end, a group of influential British political scientists were recently invited by the QAA to draw up a series of 'benchmark statements' to help give the discipline a degree of coherence. The results of this exercise make interesting reading and can found on the QAA web-site (QAA 2002).

The QAA report begins sensibly by acknowledging that the scope of the discipline is 'broad, the boundaries often being contested or in movement' and goes on to note that 'perhaps in no other academic discipline are the subject matter and approaches so much in contention and in flux'. As this present work has noted, the contested nature of Politics is an inevitable feature of a subject that deals with controversial issues that matter deeply to human beings. However Politics is defined, there will always be alternative perspectives that challenge and push the subject into further areas of enquiry. In particular, there will always be disputes concerning how we can (if at all) usefully differentiate between the social and the political, and between the private and the public. The three challenges explored earlier in this chapter all tried in their way to stretch the focus of political science into areas of society and even domestic life that previously would have been thought to be entirely non-political. Whether political scientists accept or reject such claims will in large part be determined not just by their views on politics but also their wider views on the nature of human life generally.

If you are planning to study Politics at university you will find that the nature of the curriculum, rather like the practice of politics itself, is the outcome of a series of compromises between a diverse group of academics who each hold strong views on the appropriate remit of the subject and its relationship to other areas of the academic curriculum. Academics take these issues very seriously indeed. As well as periodic external monitoring of how the subject is delivered in each institution, every Politics department will regularly review their curriculum in light of new innovations, which, as the QAA report highlights, occur perhaps more regularly in Politics than in any other subject area. To give a clearer sense of how these curriculum issues are resolved in practice by political scientists, and to provide a sense of the kind of subject matter you might encounter at university, it would be useful to briefly outline how the issue was tackled at the University of Central Lancashire in the early 1990s, where all three of the authors of this book were then employed.

Faced with the task of devising a new single honours programme in Politics, the subject team needed a clear rationale for the course that would lend coherence to the subject, whilst at the same time acknowledging its wide-ranging themes and diverse approaches. We agreed that given political science's central concern is with governance, the subject's traditional concentration upon the state was still valid, this because the state remains undeniably the most important and powerful instrument of governance and is therefore a natural focal point for political scientists concerned with how social order is maintained and resources distributed within human communities. Building upon this assumption, we devised a curriculum that organised the subject matter of Politics into three main sub-disciplines: *political theory, government* and *international relations*. Each of these sub disciplines is concerned to a large extent with analysing different aspects of the state's relationships with social and international institutions and processes. A more detailed discussion of these three sub-disciplines follows in section two of this book but briefly they can be understood as follows:

1. *Political Theory* explores the ideas of great political thinkers and looks at how different ideologies (such as **liberalism, conservatism** and **socialism**) have understood the relationship between the individual, society and the state.
2. *Government* focuses upon how individual societies organise their political institutions and decision-making processes. It is also concerned with comparing different systems of governance.
3. *International Relations* analyses the relationship between states, how order is maintained and resources distributed at a global level, and how and why poor relations between states can lead to the failure of political solutions and the use of violence.

We have found at Central Lancashire that this approach has given students a good sense of structure to their studies but has also allowed a degree of flexibility in terms of the topics covered. In recent years, for example, one of our more popular political theory **modules** explores the ideas of anarchists, who of course study the state only so they can ascertain the best method for eradicating it! Identifying the state as a useful point of focus does not in any way exclude approaches to politics such as **anarchism** or Marxism that seek to undermine the state, or those such as feminism that attempt to broaden out Politics to include aspects of our social or even private lives.

It is important to stress that the point of my discussion of how Politics has been organised at Central Lancashire (the rationale for which has also provided the structure for this text) has not been to assert this as a definitive model of how the subject should be presented, but merely to provide an example of how political science may be delivered at British universities. As the QAA report notes, it unlikely and probably not desirable that political scientists will entirely agree on a national curriculum that all students of the subject *should* study. Such creative disagreement is also evident in discussions on how political activity should be studied and interpreted. It is to these questions I shall now turn.

THE NATURE OF POLITICAL ENQUIRY

Is Politics a science or an art?

So far we have been using the term political science unproblematically, but can Politics really be scientific? The answer to this question will depend very much on who you ask and how the term science is defined. Practising politicians have often been happy to describe their occupation as an art form. The postwar Conservative politician Lord Butler defined politics as the 'art of the possible', while the nineteenth century German statesman Bismarck asserted that politics was concerned with the 'art of governing'. Both these definitions imply politics is a messy business of compromise, manipulation and persuasion that is about what works in practice rather than what can be shown to be scientifically true. Academics, however, have often been keener to establish the scientific credentials of their subject matter, lest they be accused of doing little more than asserting a series of unproven opinions and prejudices.

Most Politics scholars would be content to define their subject as scientific if by science all we mean is, in Mackenzie's (1967: 17) words, 'simply that there exists an academic tradition of the study of politics'. Politics is scientific in the broadest sense because it is a *distinctive body of knowledge accumulated over time through reflective observation and critical study.* What has been more controversial is whether Politics can be scientific in the same way as the natural sciences. Disciplines such as chemistry and physics pride themselves on being concerned with the observation and collection of objective facts. By objectivity scientists mean that their own emotive reactions or personal opinions about the nature of what they discover are unimportant: the facts as they are should speak for themselves. Scientists also seek to establish laws of cause and effect through experimentation, which can repeated by other scientists, thereby verifying the credibility of any given discovery.

It is impossible for political activity to be studied in exactly the same way as natural scientists study the laws of the physical world, such as gravity or chemical properties. This is because politics is exercised by human beings who act for a multitude of reasons, many of which are irrational or contradictory. This unpredictability means political action is much more difficult to measure than physical forces. Nor can political scientists make use of laboratory experiments to verify their claim about politics. Leaving aside the ethical questions involved with carrying out experiments on human activity, it would be impossible to replicate any given set of conditions in order to successfully repeat a particular study. For these reasons most Politics academics accept that 'they cannot make authoritative statements of the same universal validity as natural scientists' (Bealey et al. 1999: 12). While Politics cannot be studied as precisely as natural phenomenon, political science can nevertheless strive to be rigorous in its methods of enquiry, building constructively upon previous studies and thereby creating plausible explanations for political activity. It is also true to say that the differences between natural and social scientists are often exaggerated.

Firstly, like social science, natural science involves the application of theories as well as the analysis of facts. What is studied, as well as how it is studied, will be circumscribed by the theoretical assumptions that the scientist makes. Moreover, many advances in theoretical physics today are highly speculative and very hard to prove one way or another.

Consequently, there is widespread disagreement amongst natural scientists about how the world works. Quantum physicists argue about how many dimensions exist (estimates range from three to eleven), whether the origins of the universe can be explained by a single explosive event known as the 'big bang', and whether there is just one universe or a multitude of parallel universes! On a more concrete level, one only has to observe the well publicised disputes over the causes of AIDS or global warming to see that natural science, no less than social science, is characterised by heated disputes and controversies.

Secondly, the problem of objectivity is an ever-present challenge for natural as well as social scientists. Thomas Kuhn (1962) has persuasively argued that all scientific enquiry is driven by paradigms (shared beliefs about the nature of the world and how it can best be explained) that provide a defining theoretical framework for the work of scientists. These paradigms are socially determined and therefore subject to influences rather less noble than 'an objective search for the truth'. Natural scientists are human beings, of course, and prone to the same ambitions, egotism and irrationality as the rest of us. Very often a particular paradigm will come to dominate a field of scientific enquiry and alternative paradigms are systematically excluded. Personal commitment to a particular way of understanding the world may well override the scientist's desire for objectivity and inconvenient evidence which contradicts their own perspectives may be ignored. The social backgrounds of scientists are also a factor here. If leading scientists are overwhelmingly male, white and middle class (as indeed they are) this is likely to lead to particular types of study being given priority or afforded higher status.

Finally, the form science takes in any given society is in part shaped by wider societal values. This is reflected in the funding that scientists receive from government and business. The priorities of these donors may be, for example, the creation of ever more destructive weapons systems, rather than say the development of alternative sources of renewable energy such as wind or solar power. Such priorities will help determine what advances science makes and in what directions scientific knowledge is taken. The setting of these priorities and the values that underpin them are, of course, political questions and the identification and critical analysis of them is one of the most important tasks of political science.

In striving to make the study of such political questions as scientific as possible, it is important to remember that it is not only the task of Politics to explain things *as they actually are*; it is also crucial to suggest how things *ought to be*. In this sense, Politics is both a science *and* an art. As Mackenzie (1967: 20) asserts, much of political thought concerns 'the persuasive exposition of a point of view'. Political scientists aim to be creative in their arguments as well as systematic in their analyses. One of the most useful functions Politics can perform is to suggest novel solutions to the problems of governance, which hopefully may influence policy makers and participants in the political process.

Values in political analysis

Politics, then, is not just about the dispassionate study of governance in practice; it is also concerned with fundamental moral, ethical and philosophical questions. Indeed, many of the most influential political ideas have started life as assertions of a particular (and usually controversial) view of how best human beings can solve those basic dilemmas of social order and the distribution of resources. Such theoretical positions as John Locke's defence of natural rights or Marx's advocacy of communism have been hugely influential on practical politics. Locke's ideas helped lay the foundations for the American Bill of Rights, while in the postwar period numerous countries (including Russia and China) declared themselves as communist states. In attempting to develop a 'persuasive exposition' of a particular political doctrine, scholars have often utilised exaggeration and rhetoric as powerful tools of influence. On this point, Kolakowski (1978: 524) is insightful about the influence of Marx:

If Marxism has led towards a better understanding of the economics and civilization of past ages, this is in no doubt connected with the fact that Marx at times enunciated his theory in extreme, dogmatic, and unacceptable forms. If his views had been hedged around with all the restrictions and reservations that are usual in rational thought, they would have had less influence and might have gone unnoticed altogether. As it was . . . the element of absurdity was effective in transmitting their rational content.

The art of Politics is in part concerned with presenting challenging, though not always proven, theses about how the world is and how it could be if only we were to act to change it for the better. Indeed, as the next chapter will discuss, such theses, in the form of ideologies, have been the dynamic for much social change in the modern world. Rhetorical arguments will not, of course, always carry the day and part of the function of Politics is to subject theoretical assertions to the tests of logic and evidence. It is important to note, however, that *all* political scholars make value judgements about how the political world works, whether or not these assumptions are made explicit in the form of a stated ideological commitment. This is partly why a sharp distinction between the theoretical and the empirical study of politics is not helpful. All theories of politics are in part based on an observation of political realities and all empirical studies involve the application and testing of theories. Behaviouralists have been the most sceptical about the usefulness of normative theory but its **scientism** undoubtedly helped mask behaviouralism's own value assumptions. As Buxton (1985) highlights, a presumption in favour of market rather than state-led economic management and support for a limited rather than direct **democracy** was implicit in and greatly influenced the conclusions of many behaviouralist studies.

In the technical language of the discipline, the working assumptions political scientists make are sometimes referred to as *ontological positions* (assumptions about the nature of being and existence) and *epistemological positions* (assumptions about the nature of knowledge and explanation). A particular thinker's approach to these methodological questions will help shape their whole political outlook. Perspectives on such questions as human nature are crucial in moulding attitudes towards **liberty, authority** and the exercise of power. The great English political theorist Thomas Hobbes, for example, was of the view that humans are by nature egotistical, glory-seeking creatures who possessed an inherent distrust of others. This assumption laid an important foundation stone for his theory of the state, which he felt should have absolute power over its subjects, less people's selfishness led to a 'war of all against all'. Another more recent example of how a basic assumption about the nature of existence can shape a whole political approach is rational choice theory. This recently influential theory takes as its working assumption the idea that humans are rational actors who will approach politics in much the same way as they do buying and consuming products in the market place. Rational choice models of voting behaviour therefore contend that people will cast their vote for the party that comes closest to their own perspectives on politics and which best appears to represent their own personal interest, rather than voting for a party out of a sense of loyalty, tradition or altruism.

Political thinkers do not just disagree about such ontological issues as human nature; there are fundamental epistemological disputes as well. One recent approach to politics that has been influential in challenging the explanatory and predictive power of much of traditional social and political thought is **postmodernism.** Postmodernists are particularly sceptical about political doctrines that claim to have discovered the 'truth'. Nash (2000: 33) summarises the postmodern approach to methodology as follows: 'A concern with studying representations as such rather than what they are supposed to refer to; scepticism concerning the ultimate foundations of truth and value; an interest in how claims are constructed rather than whether or not they are true.'

Such arguments have led some scholars to abandon completely what they would see as the 'myth' of neutrality and objectivity. As Root (1993: 230) points out, some forms of feminism have adopted an overtly partisan approach to researching political questions:

> Value-neutrality is not an ideal for feminists currently working in the social sciences any more than it was for Marx; feminist research is openly partisan and seeks to advance the values of a community of women, just as Marx's research was partisan towards the working class.

Most political scientists would not wish to abandon completely the search for objectivity and truth. Nevertheless, postmodernism has been a useful development because it has helped political scientists think more carefully about the underlying assumptions they make. As Marsh and Stoker (1995: 288) argue, it is crucial that political scientists should 'acknowledge explicitly both their theoretical and epistemological positions'. Unfortunately, this is still far from always being the case. One of the most challenging and yet interesting tasks facing the student of politics is therefore to seek to uncover the underlying values and beliefs that shape both political ideas and practices.

SUMMARY

Politics is an extremely eclectic discipline, the boundaries and subject matter of which are constantly being shifted by new theoretical and methodological developments. In the post-war period, approaches such as behaviouralism, Marxism and feminism have broadened and deepened political science by encouraging a more systematic and critical study of a wide range of human relationships (such as mass participation in decision-making or class and gender relations) that were previously considered by students of Politics to be either non-political or relatively unimportant. Nevertheless, political science's traditional twin focus on institutional studies of the state and the history of political ideas has remained strong. Analyses of great thinkers of the past and how states are governed and relate to each other are still at the heart of Politics as it is taught in UK universities. The three sub-disciplines of *Political Theory*, *Government* and *International Relations* are therefore the subject of Part II of this book.

In recent years, Politics academics have become more self-conscious, not only about the remit of their subject, but also concerning the nature of political enquiry. Most would accept that their subject cannot be as precise a discipline as the natural sciences, mainly because Politics is concerned with human relationships and these are notoriously unpredictable! It is also inevitable that all political study begins with a set of value assumptions about such questions as human nature and the possibilities and limits of rationality. Nevertheless, Politics scholars do aim to be scientific in the broadest sense of the term, by conducting their studies in a systematic, rigorous and critical manner. It is also important to stress that Politics is not just about describing as objectively as possible how the political world operates in practice. It also has a crucial role to play in theorising new forms of governance that might improve the human condition.

FURTHER READING

Mackenzie (1967) and Blondel (1981) are interesting on the historical development of political science. The edited volume by Marsh and Stoker (1995) presents a more contemporary survey of the discipline. On behaviouralism's contribution to the subject of Politics, see Kavanagh (1983). All of the essays in Gamble et al. (1999) provide useful reminders of the ongoing importance of Marxism to the study of politics and society. A good intro-duction to the contribution feminism has made to political thought is Bryson (1992). For those looking for a readable general text that covers most of the topics taught on university Politics courses in the UK, you could do a lot worse than seek out Bealey et al. (1999). Harrison's (2001) survey of the diverse methods political scientists use to conduct their research is a useful introduction to the nature of political enquiry.

PART II
The Sub-Disciplines of Politics

Alex Thomson

4 POLITICAL THEORY

This section of the book introduces the 'content' of Political Science. Having discussed what politics is in the previous section, we can now turn our attention to what students of Politics actually study. The aim is threefold: to identify the central issues that the discipline of Politics revolves around; to assess why these particular issues are relevant: and to reveal what methods political scientists have used to analyse these issues. In other words, this section seeks to produce a broad survey of Politics, exploring the key concepts and debates contained within the subject. This is a particularly useful exercise for prospective students of Politics, as it will serve to indicate what a 'typical' undergraduate might come across if they were to study this discipline at university.

Writing a broad survey of this nature is a pretty daunting task. Similarly, new students of Politics, observing what lies before them, in terms of the many different courses and specialisms, are also often overwhelmed. How do all these aspects fit together? What is the link, for example, between Marx's theory of alienation, the powers of the Prime Minister, and diplomatic relations between the United States and Cuba? How does one go about trying to gain an understanding of all these individual issues, yet still keep a grasp of what Politics is about in a wider sense?

The best way to study Politics, in this respect, is to avoid trying to tackle the entire subject all at once. Instead, we can break the discipline down into a number of smaller, more manageable, parts. As a starting point, for instance, we saw in the previous chapter that Political Science can be usefully divided into three broad sub-disciplines: **Political Theory, Government** and **International Relations**. This is not to say that students should only specialise in one of these areas, or regard the boundaries between the sub-disciplines as rigid, but this division does help both students and professionals to gain a better grasp of what it is they are actually studying. For this reason, the three chapters of this section will also follow this pattern of division: the current chapter will look at Political Theory, Chapter 5 concentrates on Government, while the final chapter of this section introduces International Relations.

We shall look first at the sub-discipline of Political Theory because it concerns itself with the core ideas that lie at the heart of all political understanding. Before we launch ourselves into the more **empirical** fields of Government and International Relations, we first have to address the moral dimensions of political activity. We should look at the goals of politics, speculating on how things are, and how things ought to be. Key debates within Political Theory therefore include: What is an ideal **state**? Why should I obey my government? What right do I have to disagree with, or overthrow, those in authority? And what **rights** do I have as an individual within a state? These are the sort of timeless, far-reaching questions that political philosophers seek to answer. By tackling these issues in an abstract manner, scholars are free to concentrate on 'ideals' and 'utopias', contrasting these with the 'real world'. This has led to useful, imaginative and even inspirational interpretations of the political. The sub-discipline of Political Theory can thus be defined as the largely abstract critical study of the motivations, values, beliefs and principles that lie behind political behaviour.

WHY STUDY POLITICAL THEORY?

Why should we study Political Theory? Would it not be more profitable to immediately throw ourselves into empirical considerations such as the institutions of the British **constitution**, or into addressing why the Cold War ended in the late 1980s? Why bother asking philosophical questions and engaging in abstract debates when there is so much left in the 'real world' to explain? Well, such an attitude would mean missing out on what Political Theory has to offer. As this section of the chapter will demonstrate, the sub-discipline is indispensable to students of Politics for three reasons.

First, degree courses do not just exist for individuals to extend their knowledge of a particular academic discipline. As Part III of this book explains, undergraduate study also provides opportunities for personal development, in terms of transferable skills. These skills can later be applied to the workplace and to life in general. Political Theory assists this personal development through its emphasis on logic and constructing both oral and written arguments. These are communication skills that are much sought after in the job market. And it should not be forgotten that Political Theory can also be very rewarding for its own sake. Whether it is in a seminar room or down the pub, most people enjoy exercising their brain, chewing over classic philosophical questions.

Second, beyond transferable skills and personal reward, Political Theory also provides an invaluable service to the study of Politics by schooling students in the meaning of political concepts. Every area of life has its own specialist jargon. Just as football has its 'four-four-two' and its 'wing backs' and music has concepts such as 'classical', 'jazz' and 'rock', Politics uses words such as **'legitimacy'**, **'obligation'** and 'rights'. Political Theory helps us to understand what these terms actually mean. After all, states have even gone to war over differing interpretations of these concepts ('freedom' and **'sovereignty'** for instance), so it is as well that students and political scientists spend some time getting their definitions right, and learning the basic language of the discipline.

Our third reason for studying Political Theory relates to perspective, guidance and inspiration. It would be impossible to understand every political event solely on its own terms. We need ways of generalising political relationships. This is assisted by applying broader concepts such as **'democracy'** or **'socialism'** to particular cases. By identifying the common characteristics within different systems we gain a greater understanding of how the political process actually works. For instance, if a society agrees that democracy is the best way of organising a state, then it can look to democratic theory to help identify the positive characteristics of this idea, and then try to emulate them. Alternatively, it may see this concept as totally flawed and gain inspiration from the works of Marx and Lenin and try to build an alternative, communist society. Political Theory thus helps individuals to understand the world they currently live in, as well as suggesting other, potentially better ways of life.

With these issues of skills, language, perspective and inspiration in mind, it can be seen how Political Theory will contribute significantly to all Politics degrees. In a typical university programme, for example, alongside **modules** introducing Government and International Relations, first years will start off by learning what particular political concepts actually mean (power, the state, legitimacy, justice and so on). They will also investigate the common ideologies that motivate political behaviour (such as liberalism, conservatism, socialism and anarchism). Some of these concepts and ideologies will then be revisited in the second and third years, in the form of more specialist modules analysing these individual concepts in detail.

In addition to this study of 'concepts' and 'ideologies', Political Theory also concerns itself with the 'history of political thought'. This sub-field involves students looking back and critically analysing what 'great thinkers' have said about politics in the past. Degree programmes, in this respect, often have a second year 'survey' module, exploring a handful of these thinkers (Plato, Machiavelli, Hobbes, Locke, Rousseau, Mill and Marx, say). Students study the discipline's classic texts, introducing themselves to timeless debates. If they like what they read, then specialist modules may be available in the third year permitting students to concentrate on the work of just one 'great thinker'.

Following this pattern of how Political Theory is delivered at an undergraduate level, the remainder of this chapter will investigate these three sub-fields in turn. This should provide a flavour of how Political Theory is taught in British universities. We shall first look at the History of Political Thought before going on to introduce the other two sub-fields Political Concepts and Political Ideologies.

A HISTORY OF POLITICAL THOUGHT

There is no reason why students have to start from scratch when trying to understand Political Theory. Scholars have been putting forward ideas and addressing the fundamental questions of politics for centuries. In this respect, there is no need to reinvent the wheel. Newcomers to the discipline, and old hands alike, can learn much from what the 'great thinkers' have said in the past. These scholars have left a whole library of classic texts to consult (see table on p. 71). Despite each of these books being a product of its own time, it is amazing just how relevant some of these authors' thoughts are to the politics of today.

Typically, courses on the history of political thought offer a chronological survey of classic texts penned by Western scholars. They start with Plato, writing in ancient Greece, and continue through to the modern thinkers of the twentieth century. Occasionally, universities will also offer more specialist modules investigating other political traditions, particularly those of the East, but Western thinkers are more favoured. (This is a shame, since Confucius was arguing for a strict adherence to laws, due to the incorrigibility of human nature, back in the fifth century BC, and this tradition of political thought continued through to Mao Tse Tung, who was redefining socialism throughout most of the twentieth century.)

The remainder of this section will reflect the content of these university courses by taking a recklessly quick tour through a selection of Western political thinkers. It will point to the typical issues that are discussed on these Political Theory courses. Note, as we move through time, how earlier thinkers address basic questions such as What is the state? And why do I have to obey it? while later scholars move on to examine more the 'ends' of the state: justice, democracy, **equality and rights.**

Plato (c. 427–347 BC) was the first Western scholar to write systematically about politics. In the *Republic* he considers his utopian state. Plato (1987) reasoned that moral righteousness is the first duty of government and that states are established to advance the public good. Yet he argued that the public good was rarely maximised in reality. This is because whoever governs defines 'justice' and 'righteousness' in a manner that serves their own interests. They do not try to achieve true virtue. Plato's solution to this problem was for 'philosopher kings' to rule the state. This was necessary because only philosophers had the ability to ascertain what 'true' virtue was. Indeed, in its ideal form, Plato believed virtue could only be found in a parallel world that only philosophers could access. In other words, those with trained minds could transcend the world of greed and ambition and use their intelligence and reason to find this true virtue. This gave them the credentials to rule.

Plato was to change his position later, in his work the *Laws*. Lamenting that there were not enough wise men able to recognise true virtue, his idea of philosopher kings was replaced by the next best alternative: a strict set of laws that bind all within society. Whether we examine the *Republic* or the *Laws*, however, the point is that despite Plato living centuries before us, and in a completely different social context, his work addresses timeless, universal questions of politics: Who rules? (philosopher kings), How do they get their legitimacy? (by being wise), What are the mechanisms of rule? (by using reason to find true virtue) and What is the purpose of government (to advance the public good).

After the philosophers of ancient Greece, the next two thinkers that political thought courses usually turn to are the ecclesiastical scholars St Augustine of Hippo (354–430) and St Thomas Aquinas (c. 1225–74). Augustine lived just before the **Dark Ages,** while Aquinas wrote during the medieval period when politics was irretrievably intertwined with the doctrines of Christianity. Generally speaking, monarchs ruled by Divine Right during this era of religion. Divine Right is the idea that a sovereign claims their **authority** directly from God. God has chosen this individual to rule as their representative on Earth, and it therefore follows that all should obey this monarch, following God's will. After all, does not the Bible tell us: 'Let every soul be in subjection to the superior authorities, for there be no authority except by God; the existing authorities stand placed in their relative positions by God.' (Romans 13: 1). Augustine and Aquinas produced philosophical work much subtler than this crude version of Divine Right, but both did, in the final analysis, support the idea that the state gained its legitimacy from following God's will. Subjects were therefore obliged to obey the state in order that divine law be respected.

It took Niccolò Machiavelli (1469–1527) to break this stranglehold of religious ordinance. Although he was certainly against corrupt government, Machiavelli believed power, order and stability to be the true aims of politics, and these should be achieved by the most efficient means possible. In a world where humans are naturally selfish, fickle and prone to evil, Machiavelli argued that realistic methods of government should be employed. Indeed, in his book *The Prince*, Machiavelli (1981) advises rulers how to gain, use and maintain power in such a world. He suggests princes have to choose between love or fear, clemency or cruelty and liberality or meanness. He stresses that government should not be bound by morals. The only sin of politics is to lose power. So, in certain circumstances, fear, cruelty and meanness should be unleashed. Yet he does stress that, at other times, love, clemency and liberality can produce the most stable form of government.

Machiavelli's writing is a lesson in *realpolitik* (which means dealing with the world as it is, rather than how it ought to be). The means justify the ends. Interrupting our chronological survey for a moment, it is interesting to note that Friedrich Nietzsche (1844–1900) would take Machiavelli's advice to the extreme, three centuries later. Nietzsche argued that sentiments such as altruism and egalitarianism were falsehoods propagated by Christianity. Politics should not be based on pity. Instead, leaders should express egotism, strength, courage and pride in their 'will to power' (Nietzsche 1990: 44).

With the dominance of religion over politics beginning to decline from the end of the medieval period, a new *raison d'être* emerged for politics: the individual. This **liberalism** gradually ushered in the various political phenomena that we are familiar with today: **limited government**, individual rights, equality and democracy.

Thomas Hobbes (1588–1679) can just about be treated as a liberal thinker as he reasoned that states form not through divine intervention, but as a method of protecting *individual* interests. Hobbes, in his *Leviathan*, portrays the original form of human existence, before states were formed, as one of freedom. Without a government there are few restraints in this 'state of nature'. Yet this is not a good thing. Whether in self-defence or greed, Hobbes argued that individuals would infringe upon each other's freedom and violate property. With no superior authority constraining them in this state of nature, a war of 'every man, against every man' would develop, where life becomes 'solitary, poore, nasty, brutish and short' (Hobbes 1968: 185 and 186). Humans thus agreed to form states in order to provide themselves with security. One person, or group of people, was appointed to rule, to whom all citizens give their freedom in return for this security. This superior, all-powerful (sovereign) state then acted as the sole law maker and law enforcer ensuring that the brutal realities of the state of nature are exchanged for 'Common Peace and Safetie'' (1968: 227).

Hobbes' liberalism, however, ended at this point. This is because he argued that, once constituted, the state could not be legitimately removed by its subjects, unless their physical security was directly threatened. The state also had the right to eliminate any dissenting group it found amongst its population. Despite these illiberal tendencies, Hobbes' ideas did represent a major milestone in the history of political thought. He was not justifying the state in the name of God; instead he saw the state representing the aggregation of individual interests.

John Locke (1632–1704) built upon Hobbes' work. Developing the liberal tradition, Locke argued that states not only had to provide for the security of their citizens they also had to provide for their welfare. Citizens, as he put it, were entitled to look to the state for the protection of their 'Life, Liberty or Possession' (Locke 1988: 357). Indeed, Locke reasoned that since a state's very legitimacy rested on the consent of the governed, it therefore followed that these citizens were free to break their **social contract** with the state should the latter fail to serve their interests. If a state is unjust, and a better one can be constituted to replace it, then the people have a right to rebel. This, at the time, was radical thought indeed.

Locke also developed liberalism in the manner in which he argued for individual rights. He demanded religious toleration, for example, on the grounds that no man can believe or know for another. Faith should be entirely a personal matter, not to be determined by the state. Locke had thus taken the history of political thought beyond Hobbes' all-powerful state. He argued that the state should indeed protect 'life, liberty and possession' but that its power should be limited, allowing the freedom of religion.

Liberalism evolved and flourished in the eighteenth, nineteenth and twentieth centuries, and two 'thinkers' whom we can highlight as key assistants in this development are Jeremy Bentham (1748–1832) and John Stuart Mill (1806–73). Bentham's contribution derived from his thoughts on how the state could best serve the public good. He concluded that government should manufacture 'the greatest good for the greatest many'. Popularising this 'utilitarianism', Bentham argued that, for any decision, rulers should calculate the interests of all citizens and then take the path that would benefit as many of these citizens as much as possible, providing the most advantage. Thinking such as this set precedents that would eventually bring about the **welfare state**, where all citizens can enjoy the benefits of education, health care and social security. These services deliver the greatest good to the greatest many. Bentham has thus combined the idea that the state should serve the 'public good', which had been recognised since Plato's time, with the specific interests of individuals, which had not.

John Stuart Mill, perhaps the greatest exponent of later liberalism, also advocated utilitarianism. His major contribution to the history of political thought, however, was his advocacy of individual freedom. Mill believed that all individuals had the right to develop as they please, as long as their actions did not restrict the freedom of others. Just as individuals should not subjugate each other, Mill argued that

neither should the state do this. Thus governments have no
rights to restrict their citizens' free speech, their right to
association, nor their right to practise alternative lifestyles.
All should have equal rights and equal opportunities, including women. So with the maturing of liberalism, issues of
freedom, justice and equality were now firmly on the agenda
of political thought.

The history of political thought, however, does not stop
with these later liberal classic texts. Liberal ideas have developed throughout the twentieth century, and into the twenty-
first, through the work of political philosophers such as John
Rawls (1921–2002) and Robert Nozick (1938–2002). However, it is perhaps the opponents of liberalism who have
generated the most interesting political theory of the last
150 years. Karl Marx (1818–83), for example, considered
it ridiculous, as we saw in the previous chapter, that liberalism could ever deliver true freedom and equality. With
capitalism (liberalism's twin) exploiting the majority economically, this **ideology** was never going to produce the true
public good. Rhetoric about equal opportunities and liberty
was just a sham; liberalism preserved inequality. Instead,
Marx advocated the ideology of **socialism,** to be attained
through a revolution of the working class, which would
eventually lead to **communism.** We shall come back to the
ideas of socialism, along with the other modern challenges to
liberalism, namely anarchism, **feminism** and **environmentalism,** later in the chapter when we consider the study of
political ideology.

As this brief survey shows, new students of the discipline
are not alone in their interest in politics. Fine minds have been
exploring and debating the issues located at the very core of
this subject for centuries. These thinkers have left us a legacy
of classic texts that we can investigate at our leisure, or as part
of a formal university degree programme. In either case,
exploring the logic of these volumes brings considerable
rewards. Even though some of these political philosophers
lived over two thousand years ago, they still have a lot to
teach us.

Selected classic texts of Political Theory

Plato	*Republic*	c. 375 BC
	Laws	c. 360 BC
Aristotle	*Politics*	c. 335–23 BC
St Augustine of Hippo	*City of God*	c. 412–27
St Thomas Aquinas	*Summa Theologiae*	c. 1266–73
Niccolò Machiavelli	*The Prince*	1513
Thomas Hobbes	*Leviathan*	1651
John Locke	*A Letter Concerning Toleration*	1689
	Two Treatises of Civil Government	1690
(Baron) Charles de Montesquieu	*Spirit of the Laws*	1748
Jean-Jacques Rousseau	*The Social Contract*	1762
Adam Smith	*The Wealth of Nations*	1776
Alexander Hamilton and James Madison	Contributions to *The Federalist*	1787/1788
Jeremy Bentham	*Principles of Morals and Legislation*	1789
Edmund Burke	*Reflections on the Revolution in France*	1790
William Godwin	*Political Justice*	1793
G. W. F. Hegel	*Philosophy of Right*	1821
Karl Marx and Friedrich Engels	*The Communist Manifesto*	1848
John Stuart Mill	*On Liberty*	1859
	Considerations on Representative Government	1861
	The Subjugation of Women	1869
Karl Marx	*Capital*	1867, 1885 and 1894
Friedrich Nietzsche	*Thus Spoke Zarathustra*	1883
	Genealogy of Morals	1887
T. H. Green	*Lectures on the Principles of Political Obligation*	1895
Max Weber	*Economy and Society*	1922
Antonio Gramsci	*Prison Notebooks*	1929–35
John Rawls	*A Theory of Justice*	1971
Robert Nozick	*Anarchy, the State and Utopia*	1974

POLITICAL CONCEPTS

Plato, Hobbes, Marx and the like communicated their political ideas through the use of language. Indeed, this is the medium of argument that we all use. It is, therefore, imperative that we are precise in defining our terms. A debate between two people over the duties of the state, for example, would be impossible if these individuals did not share a common understanding of the word 'legitimacy'. And this is where the study of political concepts comes in. This is the sub-field of Political Theory that attempts to 'nail down' exactly what a particular word or phrase means. This, alas, is easier said than done. The definition of these concepts will change over time (as does all language), and individual scholars cannot help but impose their own values on these terms, resulting in differences of opinion. Despite this, some common ground is needed, even if constructive debate is required over the details of particular definitions. This section of the chapter therefore identifies some of the political concepts that students will be asked to analyse and understand during their degree programme.

Power, the state, sovereignty and authority

We do not have to say much about our first group of terms – **power,** the **state, sovereignty** and **authority** – as these concepts are discussed in Chapter 2. As we saw, however, these ideas provide much that a student of Political Theory can get their teeth into. For instance: What types of power are there? How can we explain the apparently contradictory concept of 'legitimate coercion' that lies at the heart of the state? And what exactly is 'authority'? (This final question is a favourite subject of debate between two of the authors of this book. The argument has rumbled on for years, but we are both still learning from this exchange.)

Obligation, legitimacy and protest

Having worked out what the state actually is, students of Political Theory can then assess the extent to which individual citizens are obliged to obey these organisations. This question of **obligation** is one of the oldest debates existing in political study. Why exactly do we accept the authority of the state? After all, most citizens can identify at least one, if not many, laws that are not to their liking. Yet, overall, they still consider it in their interests to comply with this authority. There may be a degree of socialisation (habit) in this decision, or fear of what may happen if they did not obey, but political theorists have concentrated on the idea of **legitimacy** as the key to explaining this compliance. As we saw above, Plato thought people would be happy to follow a wise ruler, Augustine and Thomas Aquinas favoured a state compatible with divine law, Hobbes' subjects support a government that provides security, Locke added liberty and property to this security, and Bentham argued that legitimacy rests on a state that can provide the greatest benefit to the greatest number. More recent thinkers have suggested other sources of legitimacy. T. H. Green (1836–82), for example, stated that government was for the common good, which obliges each individual to support it as way of helping all within society. Max Weber (1864–1920) championed legitimate states based on legal–rational institutions upholding the **rule of law**, while John Rawls (1921–2002) said people should obey the state because it is just. Of course, if states fail to meet these measures of legitimacy, there is then the question of what their citizens should do about this. Political Theory, in this respect, also concerns itself with **protest**. When can citizens revolt, and, in particular, is violence ever justified in rebellion?

Liberty, rights, social rights, justice and equality

Most modern political theorists would agree, however, that just because a state is legitimate, this does not permit it to do anything. Citizens may have given away a good proportion of their **liberty** when they moved from the state of nature, but their subsequent contract with the state does not pertain to all aspects of their lives. Individuals should therefore have **rights** guaranteeing them freedom of action in certain areas and under certain circumstances. Locke argued for the right to life, liberty and property, for example, while Mill emphasised the right to free speech, freedom of association, religious tolerance and a universal franchise. Essentially, these rights are about limiting the power of government.

Later thinkers, however, suggested that **social rights** should be added to these individual freedoms. Is not the right to welfare provision, such as health care and education, just as important as the more accepted political freedoms? Whether political or social in nature, however, rights are not properly delivered unless **equality** is observed. There needs to be a uniform rule of law providing for everyone. If there is no equality, there is no **justice**. Students of Political Theory will have ample opportunity to dissect all these terms and debate their merits during the passage of their degree course.

Democracy

Our final consideration in this brief look at political concepts is **democracy**. Western states have not only gradually developed liberal standards of legitimacy and justice since the medieval period, but in more recent times they have also established mechanisms allowing people to participate in government. This is delivered through democracy (literally meaning 'rule by the people', or more commonly understood as rule of the majority).

Throughout time, many political theorists have been extremely sceptical about this form of government. Plato, for example, described democracy as 'an agreeable anarchic form of society, with plenty of variety, which treats all men as equal, whether they are equal or not.' (Plato 1987: 315). Favouring philosopher kings, Plato questioned whether it was beneficial to give stupid citizens just as much say over law-making as the wise. Similarly, the Founding Fathers of the United States were reluctant to write a democratic constitution that would create a 'tyranny of the majority'. Consequently, they made sure that this document contained checks and balances in order to protect minority and individual rights from the wishes of the majority, or 'mob rule' (Hamilton, Madison and Jay 1961: 315–17).

But even if the desirability of democracy is accepted, questions still have to be asked. Is the only true form of democracy 'direct democracy', where every citizen votes on every decision made? Today we have representative democracy, where we select professional politicians to act on our behalf. Jean-Jacques Rousseau (1712–78) argued that this was not democracy at all: 'The English people believes itself to be free; it is gravely mistaken; it is free only during the election of Members of Parliament; as soon as the Members are elected, the people is enslaved . . .' (Rousseau 1968: 141). There is also the question of whether you can have democracy if *economic* decisions are not made by 'the people'. Liberal democracy restricts its majority rule only to the *political* domain. Socialists argue that this does not produce democracy at all. We will return to Rousseau's point of needing some form of **political participation** between elections in Chapter 5, when we look at the sub-discipline of Government, while the socialist view of democracy is investigated in just a moment.

It is essential, then, that students of Politics develop at least a basic understanding of the terms highlighted in this section. They are the key conceptual tools that allow us to make sense of the empirical world. British politics, for example, cannot be understood without referring to the ideas of 'democracy' and 'justice', while the US constitution claims to have 'liberty', 'rights' and 'equality' at its core. Whether a student decides just to take a first year survey course of this material or chooses to specialise in this area, any time spent chipping away at what these core words actually mean is effort not wasted.

IDEOLOGIES

Ideology can be described as *a lifeguiding system of beliefs, values and goals affecting political style and action.* In this sense, individuals use ideologies to help them understand and explain the world. They provide a way for human beings to synthesise the mass of information around them into something more logical and meaningful; giving them a 'world view'. Catholicism, Islam, socialism, liberalism and anarchism, for example, all serve as guides to their disciples. They provide interpretations of history, explanations of present events, and they help people to plan for the future.

Ideology, in this respect, is a socialising force. People with similar world views will cooperate to further mutual interests and defend this lifestyle against competitors. Consequently, most societies have a dominant ideology that provides the basis of social order. It is this ideology that binds state and **civil society** together, and it provides governments with their mission, coherence and, most importantly, their legitimacy. Given that ideology determines so much in the political world, these phenomena are well worth a section of their own in this chapter on Political Theory. This section will first analyse liberalism, the dominant ideology of the West, before moving on to challenges to liberalism.

Liberalism

The idea of **liberalism** can be found at the very core of society in the West. Indeed, liberalism is so ingrained in everyday life within these countries that most citizens probably don't consider liberalism to be an ideology at all. It is just how things are, and how they should be. Ever since the state ceased to be constituted in the name of God and instead became 'government for the people', liberalism has developed and prospered.

If we analyse the component parts of liberalism, the key focus of this ideology is the individual. The goal is to allow each citizen to maximise their self-development, unfettered by state interference. Certainly, there does have to be state, to protect these individuals from the 'state of nature', but government is regarded as a necessary evil. Consequently, citizens are given rights, limiting the remit of government. This prevents the state from interfering in how individuals expresses themselves, or with whom they associate. Liberalism is thus defined by its consitutionalism, its rule of law, its equality of opportunity and its tolerance. Liberalism is also noted for its partnership with capitalism, for economics is one of the areas in which state intervention is curtailed.

Challenges to liberalism

Socialism developed throughout the nineteenth and twentieth centuries as the main contender to liberalism. As we saw in the previous chapter, socialists ask how a society can ever attain an equality of opportunity if economic relations are left to the **free market**. The political rights that citizens gain under liberalism are pointless in the face of this ideology's failure to prevent economic exploitation. Socialists therefore argue that there has to be material as well as political egalitarianism for the public good to be served. They advocate that the state, rather than the market, should control the economy, working on the principle of 'From each according to his ability, to each according to his needs' (Marx 1875). Consequently, private property is natio-nalised. Socialism also advocates popular sovereignty, in that society is not regarded as an aggregate of individuals, as it is in liberalism, but instead the interests of society should be put above the needs of any one individual. All citizens are thus working for the collective whole rather than for themselves.

We should not just concentrate on the ideas of liberalism and socialism in our attempts to understand the world. For instance, it is also useful to ask if we need a state at all. Anarchists think we do not. They regard the whole concept of the state as illegitimate. Throughout history, states have caused wars, coerced whole populations, created inequality and shackled the individual. After all, what right has any person to rule over another? **Anarchism** therefore advocates sovereignty of the individual. Nobody should give away their freedom to a state. Human life is more worthwhile living in the 'state of nature'. An absence of states, anarchists propose, would not bring violence and disorder but would instead allow different sets of human relationships to develop, where cooperation would flourish, in small, self-sufficient communities. Even if students disagree with these views, anarchism is still a useful ideology to study as it concentrates these students' minds on why they personally believe the state to be legitimate.

In more modern times, **feminism** and the **environmentalism** of the Green movement have also come to challenge the dominance of liberal views. Readers can refer to the previous chapter for an introduction to feminism's contribution to Political Science. It is, however, worth reminding ourselves of this ideology's main challenge to liberalism: how can liberalism deliver the equality and opportunity for all humans that it claims, given that states exhibit tendencies of **patriarchy**, where men occupy nearly all the positions of authority and make decisions on the behalf of women? Should women not have an equal opportunity to represent themselves? Similarly, liberalism would also seem to have failed to take care of our environment. Those within the Green movement wish to restore a better balance between 'Man and Nature'. They seek to conserve and protect the environment, something that the individualism of liberalism and capitalism cannot do. These environmentalists, after all, see the Earth as only being held in trust. Current policies are therefore violating the rights of future generations. Defenders of liberalism have yet to come up with a satisfactory answer to these two challenges.

Other 'isms' that are also often studied under the broad heading of ideology are **conservatism, nationalism**, and **totalitarianism**. Some regard these movements as being not strictly ideologies in that they can be combined with any of the above systems. Both the Right and the Left, for example, have experimented with totalitarianism, notably in Hitler's Germany and the Soviet Union under Stalin (see Chapter 5 for a further discussion of totalitarianism). These concepts are, however, worthy targets of study within Political Theory as they help us to understand the values and ideas associated with such regimes. It is worth briefly looking at conservatism in more detail to illustrate this point.

Conservatism is about, as the name suggests, conserving the traditional institutions and modes of behaviour within a society. It is a philosophy that is not necessarily against change, but it argues that on no account should this reform be rapid or revolutionary. A stable 'organic' evolution of society should be the aim. The political theorist most associated with conservatism is Edmund Burke (1729–97). He warned in his *Reflections on the Revolution in France* (1968) against leaping into the unknown seeking to base political systems on abstract principles. Instead, government should rely on tradition, custom and practice because continuity brings stability. In Britain this meant supporting the monarchy, aristocracy, established Church and the existing hierarchy. Patriotism should also be a key goal. In this respect, conservatism may lack the 'vision' of liberalism, socialism or anarchism, but the above description nevertheless puts this movement squarely into our definition of ideology as *a life-guiding system of beliefs, values and goals.*

As it can be seen from this discussion, ideology is an invaluable tool of analysis for Political Scientists. It allows us to chart and categorise regimes. In many ways, ideologies gather together all the individual concepts discussed in the previous section of this chapter. They are the motivating forces that have resulted in violence within and between societies (the Spanish Civil War or the Cold War, for example), while at the same time providing the guiding principles that have brought stability and prosperity to many societies (liberalism in Britain and the United States). Whether ideologies result in social harmony or violent disorder, it is certainly true that no political scientists can ignore them.

SUMMARY

Political Theory is the sub-discipline of Politics that concerns itself with the values, beliefs and motivations of political behaviour. By thinking abstractly about these issues, the ideas that lie behind all political actions can be revealed. Political

Theory is also useful to both apprentice and professional political scientists alike in that it helps to clarify what the specialist language of the discipline actually means. To these ends, the subject matter of this sub-discipline is usually taught through three approaches. A *history of political thought* gives students an idea of how various 'great thinkers' have attempted to answer the classic questions of politics over time; *political concepts* investigates individual terms in isolation, getting to the very core of political meaning; while the study of *ideologies* demonstrates how these abstract concepts can be used as blueprints to support or challenge existing or prospective societies. In short, it is from Political Theory that scholars of the discipline gain their basic building blocks of analysis. It is from these foundations that the more empirical study of Government and International Relations has evolved.

FURTHER READING

For those readers wanting to learn more about the history of political thought, a classic collection of essays on the 'great thinkers' has been put together by the BBC (1995). Hampsher-Monk (1992) would provide a good supplement to this, going into more detail about political thought from Hobbes through to Marx. It is also rewarding to read the actual classic texts themselves. Those by Marx and Engels (1967), Machiavelli (1961), Mill (1974), and Rousseau (1968) are particularly accessible, but these and many more of the classics can be found as (free) e-texts at www.epistemelinks.com. In terms of learning more about political concepts and political ideologies, Heywood has written two excellent textbooks, a separate volume on each element (1999 and 1998). Goodwin covers the same ground in a single volume (1997). For those of you with less time on your hands, all these people and issues can be explored quickly and efficiently by using specialised political dictionaries. Scruton (1996) is the pick of the crop, in this respect.

5 GOVERNMENT

Having sought guidance from the great thinkers such as Hobbes, Locke and Marx in the previous chapter, we now leave this more philosophical area of **Political Theory** behind. Instead, it is time to move on to the sub-discipline of Government, a much more **empirical** and practical field of study. Although Government leans heavily on the ideas discussed within Political Theory, it analyses power in a less abstract manner. It is about the domestic day-to-day politics that help shape all our lives. I have specifically used the word 'domestic' here, as political relations *between* **states** are covered by our third sub-discipline, **International Relations**, which is examined in the next chapter. **Government**, then, is *the study of domestic public institutions, social groups and movements that determine the rules of, and the distribution of resources within, society.*

It is interesting that the term 'Government' has been selected as the title for this sub-discipline of domestic politics. At first glance, this would seem to be too narrow. After all, most lay people associate the word government only with the parliaments, prime ministers and bureaucracies located at the heart of the state. In this respect, it is legitimate to ask whether this concentration on 'high' politics is enough to cover all the relevant political activity found in the domestic environment.

Certainly, as it was discussed in Chapter 1, there is a case to be made for a broader remit for domestic political science. Political relationships, after all, are ubiquitous. As we have seen, they can be found in family groups, at work, in the pub, everywhere. Indeed, as soon as two human beings get together, a political relationship starts. Feminist scholars, by pursuing this line that 'the personal is political', and that no relationship should be excused from political examination, have netted valuable results. They have shown how men have used both the public *and the private* spheres throughout history to exploit women. Students of politics, in this respect, should not be afraid to explore far beyond the state.

Yet, for every political scientist to always take such a broad approach would be wrong. It is impossible to comprehend all the political relationships found within the domestic environment. There are simply too many variables. This is why political scientists, on the whole, focus on government, for it is within these institutions that the greater part of a society's power is concentrated.

However, having decided that this domestic sub-discipline should focus on 'government', it should be pointed out that political scientists do not only investigate the institutions of state. They use the term 'government' in a much wider sense. Such scholars are potentially interested in *any* authoritative body that makes decisions, wherever this may be located within society. So, along with institutions of the state, the sub-discipline additionally encompasses political phenomena such as elections, interest group lobbying, the influence of the media, mass demonstrations and 'political culture'. In other words, Government specialists ask themselves in what manner does **civil society** influence the state, and *vice versa*? These areas, then, of the state itself and the interface between state and civil society are the two key areas of study within the field of Government.

So, with this broad definition of 'government' in mind, the present chapter will introduce the sub-discipline by asking three revealing questions: Why should we study Government? What areas of this sub-discipline are commonly taught on Politics degree courses? And what methodological approaches have scholars used to try and understand Government? Taken together, these three questions should give you a fair idea of what this sub-discipline is all about, and how this field contributes to the overall academic subject of Politics.

WHY STUDY THE SUB-DISCIPLINE OF GOVERNMENT?

Motivations for students studying Government should not solely be related to the requirements of their degree programme or just personal pleasure. Certainly, by exploring this body of knowledge individuals can develop the necessary skills of research, analysis and communication needed for this qualification (see Part III). It is also to be hoped that students will find it rewarding to gain, for its own sake, further understanding of the political. Yet, at the end of the day, there are 'higher' incentives for studying Government. These relate to two vital social requirements of any **democracy**. First, that the governed within society need to keep an eye on their governors (scrutiny), and, secondly, that citizens should make informed choices about how they are governed (participation).

In terms of **scrutiny**, the politicians and public servants that inhabit the institutions of state make decisions on behalf of all of us. Similarly, leaders within pressure groups or social clubs do the same for their members. Without scrutiny, how do we know that these leaders are actually representing our interests? Although we have entrusted these public figures with power, there is no guarantee that they will then use this power to best effect. For instance, a political party may have promised prosperity for all in an election campaign, but after it gained office it systematically began to pass laws that only favoured people of retirement age, or perhaps people who lived in the south of the country. Where does this leave the younger northerners? And how would the younger northerners know of their betrayal if there were no scrutiny of government? Scrutiny is therefore the action required to make sure that those in power keep to their promises, run government efficiently, and generally act in the 'public good'. Students and academics, by revealing the political process, nourish scrutiny, thus helping society to hold their leaders to account.

The study of Government is also vital to **political participation** within society. Should citizens find something amiss with their leaders' conduct, or they think that a policy could be improved, then these individuals will need to know how to change things. They require knowledge of government to gain access to the political system. **Lobbyists,** whose profession it is to try and influence public policy, for example, make it their business to know the institutions of government inside out. They know the personnel who hold office, and understand how these institutions interact. This knowledge enables them to gain access to the decision-making process, and, ultimately, to influence what the policy outcome will be. Ordinary citizens should follow the lobbyists' example, if they too want a say. Even at a minimal level, all adult individuals should have some knowledge of government to ensure they are making an informed decision when it comes around to selecting their political leaders in elections.

Students of Government therefore play an important role in society. Alongside professional political scientists, journalists and lobbyists, they have chosen to specialise in this field. Not every citizen has the opportunity or the inclination to do likewise. In this respect, others in society are reliant upon the specialists. They benefit from the scrutiny provided, making sure that the state is indeed acting in the public interest, and they are informed by the alternative policy options that the specialists propose. With this assistance, lay people can make informed choices when they do indeed participate in the political process, through voting or perhaps by joining an interest group. The whole concept of democracy would therefore suffer considerably if there were no students of Government.

COMMON TOPICS OF STUDY WITHIN GOVERNMENT

Having defined what the sub-discipline of Government is, and its relevance to society, this section of the chapter will seek to give prospective students some idea of what they will come across if they choose to study this field as part of their degree. As you can probably imagine, given the breadth of domestic politics, a complete list of topics that can be placed under the heading 'Government' is very long indeed. Depending on their lecturers' specialisms, students may find themselves studying anything from 'the powers of the Prime Minister' through to 'local government finance', or from 'protest groups in the United States' to 'the post-colonial politics of Cameroon'. A comprehensive survey of all these courses is beyond the scope of an introductory chapter such as this. What this section will do instead, however, is investigate four broader themes that most students of Government will encounter at university. These are: the nature of state institutions, the dispersal of power within society, public policy, and case studies.

The nature of state institutions

The most obvious place for students of Government to start their studies is with the institutions of state. This is because, as it was discussed above, it is here that the greatest concentration of political power lies. In this respect, nearly all Politics programmes will have a first year course looking at the nuts and bolts of political institutions. In the UK, this is often entitled something like 'An Introduction to British Government', and if there is space on the syllabus, the British political system may also be compared to other governments from around the world.

Through these introductory courses, it is soon learnt that laws are at the heart of state **governance**. These are the supreme rules of society that everyone must obey. Consequently, in the West, government itself is divided functionally into three separate branches that respectively make, implement and enforce these laws. The law-making component is the **legislative branch**, consisting of the two houses of Parliament in Britain, or the two chambers of Congress in the United States. A second branch of government, the **executive**, will implement the laws, with a president or prime minister at its head, while the third branch makes sure that all within society conform to these laws. This is the **judicial branch** consisting of judges and the courts.

Given that these three branches lie at the heart of all

democratic political systems, degree programmes tend to spend time exploring each of these branches in some depth. With respect to the legislative branch, for example, a number of questions are asked: Who exactly are the lawmakers? How did they get to these positions of power? What is the actual process of law-making itself (from initial ideas to binding legislation)? And how does this branch interact with other agencies of government? These, along with other avenues of investigation, build a clear picture of precisely how the legislative branch works. Similarly, questions are asked about a state's executive and the judiciary. Indeed, this investigative approach into the mechanics of the various institutions of state is also extended into regional and local government and, in the case of European Union members, into **supra-national** government as well.

Understanding different state institutions and how they work internally is important for the student of Government. It provides an indispensable foundation for further political analysis. The sub-discipline, however, is not just about providing instruction manuals for these separate state institutions. We learn far more about how governmental processes actually work if we go a step further and investigate how power is distributed *between* these different institutions, and throughout society as a whole.

The distribution of political power within government and society

It is fair to say that each country in the world is host to a unique set of political relationships. The politics of Pakistan, for example, differ considerably from those of Italy. It therefore follows that each state also has a unique distribution of power within its political institutions. Scholars of politics, however, have not been daunted by these differences. There is still much to learn from these contrasts, and, indeed, even more to be gained from identifying similarities. As a result, political scientists have attempted to categorise this distribution of power on a relative scale. At one end of the scale is **totalitarianism**, and at the other pole is **pluralism**. It is worthwhile taking a closer look at these categories, as this will introduce some of the key conceptual models used by students of Government.

Totalitarianism, pluralism and elitism

The ultimate totalitarian state would be one where political power lies in the hands of just one individual. He or she would be the sole decision-maker within this society, personally commanding all the state's **sovereignty**. Some monarchs, emperors, religious leaders or ideologues may have come close to this 'pure' form of totalitarianism in the past, but in recent times it has been impossible for one individual to govern the complex modern state alone. There has to be at least some distribution of power.

The term totalitarianism is therefore usually used more loosely. It refers to a political system where power is drained from the periphery of civil society, and concentrated instead on the central institutions of the state. An elite occupy these institutions at the epicentre of power, properly led by a charismatic and dominant individual (such as Hitler or Stalin), and these individuals will stretch the tentacles of the state into all areas of people's lives. The state directs almost everything. There will be a **command economy**, for example, where the state controls economic activity, leaving little room for free market enterprise. Factories will be told what to produce, and farmers what to grow. Similarly, mass participation will be confined to just one political party, which is tightly controlled by the elite. There is no room for an opposition. The state will also involve itself in cultural affairs, making sure that all artistic expression is compatible with the elite's all-encompassing **ideology**. The media will be state controlled, and even athletes will be trained by state institutions. In short, all public life revolves around directives emanating from the institutions at the heart of the state.

By contrast, a **pluralist state** is one where citizens have equal access to power, and all can contribute to the political decision-making process. Again, it is difficult historically to find an example of a 'pure' pluralist state. Even the city-states of ancient Greece, where all citizens could participate directly in government, were not truly pluralist as they excluded women and slaves. The 'looser' term pluralism therefore refers to states where 'there are multiple centres of power, none of which is totally sovereign' (Dahl 1967: 24). This is the complete opposite of the centralised and monolithic totalitarian state.

The multiple centres of power that Robert Dahl refers to are **interest groups**. The idea is that, in a pluralist society, competing groups will share power. Each will form an interest group attempting to influence public policy. These interests groups will then clash and bargain in open competition, attempting to gain support for their particular point of view. It is then up to the state, acting as a neutral umpire, to reconcile these differences as much as possible, building a consensus to mark the way forward.

What if, for example, an oil company applies to the state for a drilling licence on land of natural beauty? The oil company will put forward its case, emphasising job prospects and tax income, to the relevant state institution. Labour groups may also support this application, seeking employment for their members. In a pluralist society, however, the alternative view will also get an airing. Green interest groups will point to the disruption of the immediate ecosystem and the damage fossil fuels cause the environment generally. Similarly, local residents may form their own action group, voicing their concerns about pollution or heavy traffic destroying their community. Once every interested party has had its say, the government will then make a final decision, which takes into account the various interest groups' positions, but ultimately advances the overall public good. This is how pluralism works in theory.

If we are discussing how power is distributed within society, however, another school of thought that demands to be considered, alongside totalitarianism and pluralism, is **elite theory**. Proponents of elite theory believe in Roberto Michels' 'iron law of oligarchy'. This law states that every organisation, whatever its nature, 'becomes a minority of directors and the majority of the directed' (Michels 1962: 70). In other words, however enlightened (or pluralistic) a modern society may be, it will always end up with a division between the few that rule and the masses who are ruled. This is the same for all systems of state governance, whether they are socialist, liberal democratic or authoritarian. Elites will form, commanding the positions of power.

This division of labour is not necessarily a bad thing. The days of direct democracy, where all (male, free) citizens of Greek city-states could debate all the decisions of government, are long gone. Britain, for example, has a population of some sixty million people. There is no way that all the adults amongst these individuals can directly participate in the governance of the state. Reaching a consensus from all the different individual views would prove impossible, and this is assuming that all these citizens would want to participate anyway. Indeed, the economy simply could not afford to have everyone dedicating his or her time to issues of state. Consequently, most citizens are content to let a small group within society specialise in governance, leaving the others the opportunity to pursue other interests in life. This is the way it has to be: governors and the governed. As Dye and Zeigler put it, in their classic textbook *The Irony of Democracy*, 'There is no "solution" to elitism, any more than there is a cure for old age' (2000: 407).

The key to a healthy democracy, however, is the extent to which this inevitable elite occupying the institutions of state remain responsive to the masses. The danger is that a gap will develop between the governors and the governed, and this elite will use the trappings of state to further their own interests, rather than pursuing the wider public good. Members of this elite are often, after all, already untypical of the masses. They are individuals who usually enjoy privileged backgrounds in terms of wealth, status, education and knowledge. Yet these characteristics do help them govern. Indeed, some argue that this elite is actually more committed to democratic values that the masses themselves, who are 'fatally vulnerable to tyranny'

(Dye and Zeigler 2000: 410). History has shown, in this respect, that it is the middle classes amongst all social groups who champion democracy and liberal freedoms the most.

Fortunately, however, the masses do not have to rely solely on the elite's public spirit to safeguard democracy. Two political mechanisms exist to help increase pluralism. For those lucky enough to live under democratic systems, provisions of the 'separation of the powers' and 'participation' help to maintain a healthy balance between elite and masses. Both these mechanisms are worth looking at in more detail, as they are the key to determining how power is distributed within a society. They are also common topics of academic study found on most university degree courses.

Separation of the powers

A **separation of the powers** is precisely what does *not* happen in a totalitarian political system. Instead of centralising the state, focusing all political authority on a single point, democratic governance, through this separation of the powers, tends to disperse sovereignty, sharing it out amongst several locations. This pluralist idea narrows the chance of any single part of the state, society or the ruling elite becoming too powerful and progressing down the road to tyranny.

In the US system of government the separation of powers is very obvious. Indeed, the whole structure of the state is based upon the principle of **limited government**. This means that some sovereignty has never been given over to the state in the first place. It remains reserved for the people and out of bounds for government. US citizens therefore enjoy well-defined liberal freedoms, spelt out explicitly in their Bill of Rights. Consequently, no administrative elite in Washington DC has ever been able to infringe upon an American's right to free speech, for example, or their right of assembly. British citizens also enjoy comparatively high levels of liberal freedoms, yet this is more down to political tradition rather than legally sanctioned limited government. It is by convention that Parliament has shown self-restraint and has chosen to limit the areas it legislates upon. It too respects the individual **rights** of its citizens. Power is thus divided between state institutions and the people.

A separation of the powers, in addition to this government/people division, also requires a dispersal of power *between* state institutions. This is why most Western states have several geographical jurisdictions of authority. Again, we can compare the United States to Britain. The United States is a federal republic. That is to say, power is divided between one national government and fifty other separate provincial authorities (the individual states of the Union). Although the balance of power between these different locations has ebbed and flowed over time, the separate component governments have always had different responsibilities and jurisdictions. Louisiana's state government, for example, has sovereignty over areas such as local education, law enforcement and welfare provision, while Washington DC concentrates on more strategic, national issues, particularly those of interstate commerce, defence, foreign affairs and international trade. The British political system also has several geographical jurisdictions of authority. Recently added to its long-established local governments, and the 'off and on' government of Northern Ireland, have been a Scottish Parliament and a Welsh Assembly. Local authorities such as these help to disperse power amongst the different institutions of the state.

Going beyond a division of power between the state and the people, and between several geographical jurisdictions, is a third tier of separation. This is within central government itself. We have already seen, earlier in the chapter, how democratic administrations tend to divide into three distinct branches: the legislature, the executive and the judiciary. This, once again, is a safeguard against tyranny. The different branches actively scrutinise each other.

In Britain, for example, should a Prime Minister be perceived to be becoming too powerful, Parliament has the ability to remove him or her. This safeguard of the legislature being able to remove the chief executive actually happened in the United States during 1974. Richard Nixon was forced by Congress to resign over the Watergate affair. The President had become implicated in trying to cover up a politically inspired burglary of the opposition Democratic Party's campaign office. The mechanism worked. One branch of government 'policed' the other when its leader had overreached his authority. Other similar checks and balances can be found throughout democratic structures of government. There are even safeguards internally within single branches. The legislatures of both the United States and Britain, for instance, have two chambers. This is so one can act as a sentinel against any potential damaging acts of the other.

Many undergraduate courses examine these separations of power in detail, assessing how, institutionally, democracy is safeguarded. Often the subject will be introduced by analysing and comparing different **constitutions**. Constitutions are, after all, the key to understanding a state's political system. This is where the formal rules of political engagement and the structure of government are rooted. The United States, for instance, has a written constitution that lays out in black and white the powers retained by the people in terms of individual rights, the powers reserved to the fifty states, and the powers allocated to the national government in Washington DC.

Britain, of course, famously has an 'unwritten' constitution. This is to say that its rules of political engagement are not to be found in a single authoritative document but are instead drawn from several sources. These include the laws passed by Parliament, how these laws have been interpreted in the courts, and conventions that have developed over time. Despite what some regard as hangovers from the past, such as a role for the monarch and the fact that our individual freedoms are only protected by convention (rather than a formal Bill of Rights), this constitution has served Britain well over time. Its flexibility has allowed the political rules to adapt alongside society itself over the centuries, providing a remarkably stable political history when compared to the political violence experienced by neighbouring societies.

Despite this relative 'domestic tranquillity', students who choose to study the British constitution today are thrown into a far-reaching debate, questioning the merits of such a constitution. Has the British Constitution reached its sell-by date? Is it time to exchange some of the flexibility currently enjoyed, in return for citizens gaining more formal inalienable rights? By addressing such questions, students are transported to the very epicentre of the British state, scrutinising its ability to separate the powers.

Participation

Democracy, however, should not just be reliant on a separation of the powers for its survival. Individual rights, regional distributions of authority, and institutional checks and balances are essential, but beyond this, government of the state has to be a two-way process. If the elite who occupy the institutions of state are indeed doing this 'for the people', then the demands and ideas of the masses must permeate through to the decision-makers. It is imperative, therefore, that citizens have the opportunity to participate in their own governance.

The most obvious mechanisms to provide this participation are elections. Such polls allow citizens to select between competing political elites, determining the general outline of public policy in their country. Voters may also be asked to make direct political decisions through referenda. Elections are thus the key element of democratic government.

Given the importance of elections, political scientists have made considerable efforts to analyse elections throughout the world, and consequently many universities offer undergraduate courses in electoral studies. The content of these vary considerably. Students may be asked to dissect particular polls, weighing up the explanations for victory and defeat. How did Labour lose in 1992 yet win in 1997? Alternative **modules** debate the relative merits of the different types of polling systems available. Would Britain be better off with **proportional representation** (PR), and, if so, which form of PR should be selected? Similarly, questions can be asked about the level of choice offered in polls. After all, even totalitarian states hold elections. So, what is the 'x-factor' that actually provides an opportunity for *genuine* participation? Clearly, the regular elections that have brought Sadaam Hussein 90-plus per cent approval since he came to power in Iraq cannot be compared to presidential polls in the United States. But why exactly is this? An answer to this question should focus on the lack of liberal freedoms in Iraq, such as the rights to free speech and assembly, and freedom of the media. Polls in Iraq also lack a choice between competing ideas and candidates.

However, some would argue that even the party system in the US offers too little choice for voters. With the Republican and Democratic parties being so similar in outlook, does this explain why so many Americans, around half, simply choose not to vote for a president in the self-proclaimed 'greatest democracy on the planet'? And while we are in this part of the world, why was it that Al Gore lost the US presidential race to George W. Bush in 2000, despite winning a majority of the votes cast? Likewise, how do politicians raise the millions of dollars they need to attain office in the United States (and elsewhere), and should money play such a key role in a democratic system? There is no shortage of interesting questions for students of electoral politics to get their teeth into.

But is participation just about voting? What happens in the time periods between elections? Should we just be passive citizens until called upon to vote again? Joseph Schumpeter, an elite theorist, proposed 'that the people' are, and can be, nothing more than 'the producers of governments', a mechanism to select 'the men who are able to do the deciding' (Schumpeter 1976: 296). But surely a good democracy goes beyond mere *selection* and rests on *influence* as well? For this reason, political scientists also investigate participation via other methods. Political parties and interest groups rank highly in these 'other methods' and are thus widely studied within the sub-discipline of Government. The fact that the rest of this section, for the sake of brevity, will concentrate on just these two types of organisation, however, should not distract the reader from other, less institutional influences on the state. The media, public opinion, demonstrations and political culture also help to shape the manner in which civil society is able to sway public policy decisions. All these non-electoral methods of participation, and more, crop up regularly as issues of study on Politics degrees.

Political parties play an indispensable role in all Western democracies. As well as being the bodies that train politicians, offer constituents alternative choices at election time and, when in power, provide a mechanism for coordinating government across the separate institutions of the state, parties also offer a vital source of participation in the political process. They are the method in which individuals within society can aggregate their demands. In other words, people of like thinking can come together and compete and compromise amongst themselves in order to build a wider political programme. They can do this within an existing party or form a new one of their own. And should they win enough support for their proposals, they can then take their programme into government. Demands that originate in civil society, should they prove popular, are thus transported, via political parties, into state structures. Elite theorists, however, remind us that parties too are subject to the Iron Law of Oligarchy. Consequently, political scholars study these organisations very closely, making judgements over which way the policy ideas and demands are flowing. Does the mass membership influence the actions of the leadership, or is it the other way around? It may not just be one-party states where the leadership tends to dictate policy to the party members.

Interest groups, or pressure groups, are similar to political parties. They too offer an opportunity for political participation, as they provide a link between state and civil society, and they seek to influence public policy. The difference between the two, however, is that interest groups, unlike political parties, are not seeking to capture power themselves. Instead of their members standing for political office, they attempt to change policy indirectly through lobbying state institutions and mobilising public opinion.

Pressure groups represent issues as diverse as the interests found within civil society itself. Business corporations, for example, have their own lobby organisations, as do workers with their trade unions. Similarly, on the question of abortion, there are pro-life and pro-choice groups, and on animal rights both pro-hunt and anti-hunt movements exist. All told, there are no shortage of interest groups present in Western democracies and these act as valuable vehicles for citizens to participate in policy debates between elections.

Indeed, interest group activity can be depicted as pluralism working at its best. This theory portrays each issue generating multiple lobby groups to represent shades of opinion. These groups will then compete, putting across their case, and after everyone has had their say, the neutral state will then make a decision, taking into account the arguments presented, public opinion and the public good. There is thus a healthy competition between the different interests in society, with all the participants committed to peaceful channels of conflict resolution. Seasoned political scientists investigating these pressure groups, however, dig below the surface of this apparent equilibrium of interests. Is there really pluralism at work here? Many scholars, for example, would point to the fact that corporate interests have far more resources to expend on presenting their case to government than, say, environmental protestors. They also often have better personal contacts with decision-makers within the state. Any student who studies interest group activity soon finds out that even those societies that most closely resemble the ideal model of pluralism operate on a far from level political playing field. This, again, is another fascinating topic for undergraduate study.

Public policy

Our third selected topic of Government, **public policy**, follows on naturally from the 'institutions' and 'power dispersal' issues discussed above. This is because the policy process is carried out in institutions and the distribution of power will determine what this policy will actually be. In this respect, policy can be regarded as the 'end product' of politics. It establishes a society's laws and it resolves how resources are to be allocated. It is only right, then, with so much at stake, that public policy is another key area for students of Politics to study.

Specialist modules abound within the field of public policy. A major concern of any modern society, for example, is education. Typical courses in this area will look at the history of education policy, the networks and influences that have developed around this decision-making field, suggested reforms to the existing policy, and, indeed, what the current policy actually is. Why, for instance, is it that there appears to be less money available for students of higher education today than in the past? How has education policy evolved to this present position? Would a graduate tax be a useful reform? Who would be involved in making such a decision? These are typical of the kinds of questions that are asked amongst policy specialists. Beyond education, studies in health and housing are also common, as are modules on state benefits. Transport provision may be your thing, or perhaps how the state has intervened in the arts. I have even come across a module entitled 'The Politics of Football'. This looks at how the game is administered around the world and how state initiatives have emerged in an attempt to combat hooliganism and racism amongst supporters. So, whether it deals with one specific field or wider issues such as the welfare state as a whole, or nationalisation versus privatisation, there is something for everyone within the public policy area of Government.

Case studies

Case studies, the final common topic of study in this section, are perhaps the most prevalent modules on university Politics programmes. These provide an opportunity for students to put into perspective some of the more abstract ideas they have come across during their studies. Whether it be the pluralism or elitism mentioned above, or the theoretical material discussed in the last chapter, concepts are of most use when applied to the 'real' world. Understanding is gained by using these concepts to help explain actual political events or trends.

These case study modules often come in the form of 'country studies'. This allows a student to investigate how 'real life' governments work, as well as observing how institutions come together to form the state. If our country study is France, for example, we can see how delegates work in the National Assembly and how the president operates from the Elysée Palace. We may also be interested in how the French judicial system works, enforcing the rules of the state, or how local government is implemented through the *départements* of that country. Judgements can also be made over how power is distributed within this society. Is France a pluralist or totalitarian state? Does this country have a centralised power structure? What level of mass participation is there? What electoral system is in use? What are the key elements of public policy in France? The questions are endless and much can be learnt about how governments operate in general from a national case study such as this.

Many students during their university career take a number of these 'country modules', building their knowledge of the world and allowing comparisons to be made. Above, we compared the UK briefly to the United States, but this can also be repeated with the governments of Western Europe, or wider afield in the former socialist bloc. Comparisons with Third World societies are even more rewarding as here we come across variables such as the power of the military, ethnic ties, non-electoral forms of **legitimacy**, and different ideologies. The world is indeed your oyster if you chose to study the sub-discipline of Government. Whether you concentrate on how institutions work, the distribution of power, constitutional checks and balances, participation, or public policy, it is genuinely rewarding to discover how the political process works.

APPROACHES TO THE STUDY OF GOVERNMENT

Another informative way of introducing the sub-discipline of Government is through highlighting the different approaches scholars have used to study this subject. Approaches are all about trying to tie disparate individual areas of research together. They seek to build an overall understanding and method of study. By advancing these expansive frameworks, political scientists are suggesting potentially rewarding ways in which evidence can be gathered and analysed. Such approaches, in the case of Government, fall broadly into two schools: the **institutional** and the **structural**. A brief look at each of these can convey much about how scholars perceive this sub-discipline.

The institutional approach

As we established above, the study of state institutions lies at the heart of Government. In this respect, the traditional approach towards the sub-discipline has revolved around dissecting these institutions. This process of analysis is often associated with the **Public Administration** field of the discipline and encompasses much of what has been identified above. Public Administration specialists will therefore examine the different branches of government, explaining precisely how these organisations work and interact, and how they impact upon **public policy**. They are interested in all aspects of state organisation, from the lofty offices of central government through to the bureaucratic agencies of state, all the way down to the lowly sub-committees of parish councils. Researchers of Public Administration provide society with much that it needs in terms of scrutinising government, as well as suggesting how citizens can participate by engaging these institutions.

We have already seen, however, that individual institutions are not studied in isolation. It is often useful to compare one institution with another from a different country. This is the field of **Comparative Government**. We can compare, for example, the US **executive branch** with the French executive, or the British civil service with the bureaucracy of a one-party state such as Libya. In doing so, we learn not only about the two systems of government concerned, but by analysing the similarities and differences we also often gain an extra reward. Indeed, in many university departments, the study of just one foreign political system is also termed 'Comparative Government'. This is because students can use the knowledge gained from the external state to make judgements about their own system of government. Does Germany, for example, with proportional representation, have a better electoral system than Britain? Or perhaps Russia is better off with its strong president rather than our cabinet style of government? We can learn much from such international comparisons. As Woodrow Wilson, a president of the United States (1913–21), but formerly a university professor, argued, 'our institutions can be understood and appreciated only by those who know other systems of government' (Wilson 1899: 34).

Another field of the institutional approach is **Policy Analysis**. This framework concentrates specifically on the decision-making process. Much can be learnt from investigating how a policy is made because governments are not monolithic. Policy instead stems from numerous decisions made within different institutions at different times and at different levels of hierarchy. Take a hypothetical case of a Prime Minister announcing that Manchester has been selected as the location for a new state-funded national stadium. He or she did not decide this alone. Policy analysts will ask questions such as: How did this issue get on the governmental agenda in the first place? What other locations were considered for the stadium? Which institutions of government were responsible for gathering and presenting the information to the final decision-makers? Was this information accurate? And, once the policy was decided and Parliament had passed legislation, were Parliament's wishes carried out effectively? Policy analysts also make judgements about whether a policy was a success or not.

As well as highlighting how institutions work and offering scrutiny, in terms of making sure correct decisions have been made, Policy Analysis also reveals information about 'bureaucratic politics'. This is necessary because individual institutions often compete with each other within government. If we consider our national stadium example again: it may have been that the Welsh Office was arguing for Cardiff as the host city; the Department of Transport favoured Peterborough because these officials had long lobbied for a high-speed rail link to this location, and a public project such as this would further their case; the Department of Culture and Sport backed London as this could be the centrepiece of its desired Olympic bid; and the Treasury supported Newcastle upon Tyne because this was the cheapest proposed site. Add to this departmental wrangling, a number of MPs and local councils demanding that the stadium should be built within their constituencies, and the complexity of any one decision becomes apparent. Government is certainly not about one person making one decision. Instead, policy output will be determined by numerous decisions made at different levels of government. The task of the policy analyst is to make sense of this complex network by identifying as many of the inputs and decision-taking moments as possible. Once this has been achieved, judging the appropriateness of a policy and assessing how power is dispersed within the institutions of state becomes all the more easy.

It was the institutional approach and its analysis of state organisations that first led Politics to develop as a separate academic subject in its own right. Such an approach distinguished it from the longer-established disciplines of History and Law. Since this time, the development of the Public Administration, Comparative Government and Policy Analysis fields have developed Politics considerably further. Much has been learnt. For instance, all three of these sub-fields have started to look beyond the state. The traditional state institutions are still their main focus but most political scientists now agree that they have to employ a wider remit to include influences on public policy-making originating from civil society.

This broader approach can be illustrated by returning to our national stadium example. The decision-making process would not have been contained entirely within state institutions. Influences from civil society would also have impacted on the deliberations. What access to the process, for instance, did business corporations have? Which companies lobbied for which cities, and why? What contacts did the potential building contractors have with the relevant state institutions? What locations did the concerned sports federations demand? Did the Football Association and the UK Athletics governing bodies agree on what they wanted from a national stadium? How influential was public opinion? Whatever the decision is, state officials rarely act in a vacuum, free from external societal pressures. Consequently, the study of Government also requires that one looks beyond the state.

The structural approach

The **structural approach** to the sub-discipline of Government attempts to identify and analyse sources of power external to state institutions (but still within the domestic political arena). In this respect, 'structuralists' go beyond prime ministers, parliaments and constitutions to concentrate instead on forces located within civil society. In particular, these scholars seek to identify those 'external' organisations that interact with state institutions, attempting to either influence, or possibly to control, public policy. In doing this, they highlight influences on politics that the institutional approach tends to ignore or under-represent. Not being afraid to borrow from the disciplines of sociology and anthropology, these 'structuralists' or 'political sociologists' have revealed, significant influences that challenge, or collaborate with, state institutions. These influences, despite being located in civil society and not the state, are thus very much part of the overall domestic political process. Indeed, in some cases, there is even compelling evidence to suggest that these structural forces are crucial powers that lie 'behind the throne' in their respective countries.

But what exactly are these civil society-based forces? Well, most obviously they include social groups with economic power. Relatively rich individuals or organisations may mobilise from within civil society in an attempt to set the **political**

agenda. They will use their wealth to gain access to, and possibly to dictate to, the institutions of state. Beyond these economic groups, other influential social forces can also be found. Prominent are those organising along the lines of ethnicity, gender, race, religion or ideology. A student of Nigerian politics, for example, would be negligent if they concentrated solely on this country's state institutions whilst ignoring the social influence of ethnic groups on political events. The study of Northern Irish politics demands the same kind of considerations. Elsewhere, to understand political events in India, one must not just analyse the executive in New Delhi or the competing political parties. Here, it is religion that is a key variable.

Marxism and **feminism** are two commonly used tools of analysis amongst political scientists. They illustrate the structuralist approach well. As we saw in the last two chapters, many Marxists place social class at the heart of political relations. The bourgeoisie, using their superior economic power, have extended their domination beyond civil society and have captured the institutions of the state for themselves. The state therefore acts as an 'executive of the bourgeoisie', protecting the ruling class's interests, thus perpetuating their dominance. Marxists believe it is therefore naïve to talk about the prime minister or Parliament ruling. Instead it should be recognised that forces operating from within civil society control state institutions.

Feminists also share this structural approach. They argue that it is pointless analysing the intricate politics of the state unless one first recognises that all these institutions are subject to a greater social influence of gender discrimination. Whatever the machinations of government, social pressures emanating from civil society have already determined that the laws of the land will collectively benefit male interests at the expense of women.

In short, then, what the structural approach attempts to do is to put the institutional approach into some kind of wider perspective. Only in this manner will the study of Government be drawn away from being merely the 'science of the state'.

The sub-discipline should instead identify and analyse *all* the major variables that influence the governmental process, including those that originate outside the state and from within civil society. Only by combining these institutional and structural approaches is it possible to gain a true understanding of politics.

SUMMARY

Government, then, is the sub-discipline of Politics that concentrates on the domestic arena. It seeks to analyse how laws are made and how resources are distributed within society. This is achieved through studying institutions. In this respect, *state* organisations are the key focus of the sub-discipline, as this is where a greater part of a society's political power is concentrated. Given that this is the case, university Politics degrees spend a good deal of time investigating these institutions of state. British students, for example, have ample opportunity to learn about the 'unwritten constitution', Parliamentary sovereignty, the powers of the Prime Minister, the role of the civil service, how local government works, and the impact of the European Union on Westminster's governance. They will also become familiar with the decision-making processes of public policy. Courses will offer explanations relating to how policy is made while also encouraging students to make judgements over whether correct decisions have been taken in the past. The knowledge gained of the British state and its public policy can then be compared to other state systems found around the world, and *vice versa*.

This focus on state organisation, however, is not to say that other, non-state, institutions can be ignored. After all, broader studies of Government, which have concentrated on the interface between state and civil society, have found many influences on public policy emanating from deep within civil society. This means that, added to the institutions of the state, students of Government also look at factors such as elections, political parties, interest group activity, the impact of the media, political culture and other socially based political forces. All these civil society organisations have a leading role in the political process. Students are therefore encouraged to take both an institutional *and* a structural approach to the sub-discipline of Government. The reward for this combined approach, it is to be hoped, will be twofold. First, in the shorter term, the securing of a good degree result and the associated development of transferable skills. And, in the second place, an accumulated knowledge that will continue to be relevant beyond a student's university days, in terms of an ability to scrutinise government and to participate within the political process.

FURTHER READING

Country studies are the most rewarding way to start learning about Government. Numerous textbooks are available, but two that stand out are Jones et al. (2001) and McKay (2001) which look at state institutions and societal influences respectively in Britain and the United States. Two equally well written books that cover the same ground but in an entertaining and more controversial manner are Kingdom (1999) on the UK system, and Dye and Zeigler (2000) for the US. For those of you who want to travel further afield, getting away from the Western liberal democracies, studying the politics of the Third World can be very rewarding. Clapham (1985) provides an excellent introduction to the Third World as a whole, while my textbook on Africa is specifically designed to expose undergraduates to Government in a non-Western environment (Thomson 2000). Moving on to the different methodological approaches found within the sub-discipline, Marsh and Stoker's (1995) edited book is an excellent survey of the different ways political scientists 'do' politics. And finally, for a closer look at the comparative method, Hague and Harrop (2001) provide a good survey juxtaposing a number of states, while Faulks (1999) is an accessible introduction to some of the ideas that 'structuralists' have brought to the sub-discipline.

6 INTERNATIONAL RELATIONS

Having looked respectively at **Political Theory** and **Government** in the previous two chapters of this section, it is now time to turn our attention to the third sub-discipline of Politics, that of **International Relations**. This will complete our brief tour through the basic 'content' of political study.

A traditional definition of International Relations relates to *the interaction between, and amongst,* **states**. So, if the previous chapter on Government was about domestic Politics, International Relations analyses the external environment. It concerns itself with conflict and cooperation between states, as well as the nature of the **international system** itself. Scholars therefore concentrate on issues such as **diplomacy, war**, foreign policy and regional cooperation. As a result, *state* actions are very much the key focus within this traditional view of International Relations.

A case, however, can be made for a broader definition of this sub-discipline. Many academics within the field also regard non-state actors to be worthy of study. Going beyond the narrower power politics between states, they analyse other transnational issues: corporate activity, Third World debt, and terrorism, for example. This much broader definition of International Relations (IR) can go as far as encompassing *the study of all political relationships that cannot be explained purely within the context or jurisdiction of one state.*

This chapter, in seeking to convey the full flavour of IR, will utilise both this wider and the more traditional definition of the sub-discipline. In this respect, a good introductory survey can be structured around three basic questions: Why is it worth studying International Relations? What are the common topics addressed within IR courses at university? And how have scholars approached this subject in the past? In combination, these three questions should give you a fair idea about what International Relations is all about, providing a firm foundation for any further study you may wish to pursue in this area.

WHY STUDY INTERNATIONAL RELATIONS?

Political relationships do not stop at the water's edge. They are little restrained by international boundaries. Given that individuals, organisations and states pursue interests within other societies, it follows that international political relationships are generated. It is fair to comment, therefore, that political activities are just as much a part of this external arena as they are the domestic environment.

In this respect, most of the motivations for studying International Relations are identical to those mentioned in the previous chapter exploring the sub-discipline of Government. Beyond being worthy of study for its own sake, understanding the politics of the international environment helps us to recognise interested parties and can assist the process of peaceful conflict resolution between these groups, helping to avoid violence. It also provides individuals with skills and knowledge, enabling them to keep an eye on their leaders, making sure that they are indeed acting for the public good.

It could be argued, however, that the need for people to understand international relations is even greater than to comprehend domestic politics. This is because the consequences of ignorance in this international sphere are acute. Wars between states are devastating. Indeed, a serious collapse of the international order could precipitate the end of civilisation altogether. Just one modern submarine has the equivalent firepower of three times that used by all sides during the Second World War. In this respect, it is the desire to understand war that has done most to foster the study of International Relations.

Although many in the past have considered the politics of the external environment, starting with Thucydides (1954) in ancient Greece some twenty-four centuries ago, it was the aftermath of the First World War that spurred on International Relations as a modern academic discipline. With some nine million combatants left dead on the battlefields of Europe, scholars made haste in trying to understand the international system, attempting to conceive global institutions that could regulate conflict resolution in a peaceful manner. An alternative to war was sought as nobody wanted to live through such carnage again. Similar injections of activity and the development of the discipline were experienced after the Second World War, during the Cold War, and with the advent of the 'New World Order'. As James Lee puts it, 'The formal study of IR was thus a child of necessity: human survival' (Lee 1994: 28).

It is not just in terms of violent conflict, however, that the consequences of international relations are acute. There is also the structural violence brought about by inequality across the globe. Millions of deaths occur each year in the Third World, many of which could be avoided if there were greater political and economic parity within the international system of states. This has motivated many within the field of IR to try and identify an alternative international system, providing better opportunities for all human beings, wherever they live.

The violence and poverty highlighted above are realities of our world today. Given that the very nature of the current international system aids and abets such realities, this makes IR a subject truly worthy of study. Indeed, International Relations, for these reasons, is a discipline that demands to be studied.

COMMON TOPICS OF STUDY WITHIN IR

Most scholars, then, study International Relations for a combination of the motivations mentioned above. There is a feeling that one can make, however modest, a contribution to the debate over how the world system ought to be managed. But what exactly will you be asked to study? Should you too seek to engage this debate and choose a university degree involving the study of IR? What are the common themes that apprentices to this subject consider? This section of the chapter highlights five major topics within the sub-discipline, most, if not all of which, you will come across on a such a degree course. The issues selected are: the international system itself, the conduct of international relations, empirical case studies, international organisations and the international political economy.

The international system

The first concept a student of IR has to grasp is the nature of the **international system**. As we saw in the Political Theory chapter of this section, throughout history human beings have come together to form societies, most with an accompanying government exercising political **authority**. Individuals give away some of their freedom to these state structures and accept this higher authority in return for benefits of security and economic welfare. State authority has thus, over time, maintained a degree of stability in the domestic political arena.

Yet where is this higher authority providing stability in the international system? Should there be a clash of interests between states, to whom can these states turn? Unlike the domestic environment, there is no supreme authority in the international sphere that can step in to prevent conflict, provide arbitration or promote cooperation. It is up to the individual states to manufacture this amongst themselves. In short, this creates a very different political system *between* states to those found *within* states.

Essentially, the international system is anarchic. This does not mean necessarily that it is chaotic, but it is, in the strict meaning of this word, 'without government'. We are reminded, once again, of Hobbes' 'state of nature', discussed in Chapter 4. That is to say, given the lack of a higher authority, all states within the international system are self-reliant, with only their own power to protect themselves and promote their interests. With no 'world government' ruling over them, states are free to pursue their own destiny. Only self-restraint and the limits of the **power** at their disposal hinder a state's ambitions. There is no supreme legislature, no single law enforcer, and, indeed, no **rule of law**.

Despite this anarchy, however, and the potential for Hobbes' war of 'all against all', violent conflict is not the most common form of state interaction. Mutual self-interest dictates that at least some level of cooperation and trust must be generated. States, therefore, will usually observe the 'civilised' norms of international relations in an effort to preserve the peace and foster mutually beneficial economic and social exchanges.

One of these 'norms' is the idea of **state sovereignty**. Indeed, a respect for state sovereignty lies at the very core of understanding the modern international system. Sovereignty, in this sense, involves *the recognition of the independence, territorial integrity and inviolability of a state*. Essentially, in order to preserve the wider peace, this concept requires a mutual respect and a basic equality of status amongst states. This dictates that no state should meddle in the internal affairs of its neighbours.

This notion of state sovereignty can be traced all the way back to the 1648 **Treaty of Westphalia**. The first half of the seventeenth century had seen Europe tearing itself apart in a series of religious wars. Popes and Catholic kings were constantly waging war against Protestant princes, and *vice versa*. The aim was to protect fellow worshippers who found themselves under the authority of a state favouring a different domination. The Treaty of Westphalia ended this political instability by agreeing that a state's sovereign would now be the sole representative of their territory. This head of state would thus select their country's religion, and this decision had to be respected by all other states party to the Treaty.

In effect, the Treaty of Westphalia set the norm that a state consists of defined territory, each territory has just one recognised government, and that this government has sole political authority over the inhabitants of the territory. Stability would now be increased in the international system because just as state A would recognise the sovereignty of state B, state B would return this compliment to A. All states in the system thus became bound together by this mutually beneficial concept. So, whether we are talking about a large or small, a weak or powerful state, each unit in the international system is accorded this same sovereign status. No state has the right to intervene in the domestic jurisdiction of another.

So, here we have the key reality of international relations: unlike domestic politics, the international system is anarchic. Perpetual violence, however, has not been the result of this absence of a supreme authority. The recognised concept of state sovereignty has filled the breach. This gives us an international system consisting of numerous independent territories. Each of these is led by a single recognised sovereign government, which competes and cooperates with its neighbours externally. Internally, however, states enjoy unfettered control over their domestic jurisdiction. The world is a more peaceful place as a result. This is, at least, how it is meant to work, but for perhaps a more realistic exploration of how states interact, we can now move on to explore the conduct of international relations.

The conduct of international relations

Given the anarchic character of the international system, there can be little doubt that power is the key factor in determining relations between states. In its most naked form, war is the result. One state will pursue its interests by military force at the expense of another. States, however, will go to great lengths to avoid war. More often they pursue their interests through persuasion and cooperation, underpinned by diplomacy. The conduct of international relations can thus be seen as an application of power via the practice of war and diplomacy. Both these phenomena will be discussed in more detail.

Technically, if we use Bernard Crick's (2000) definition,

discussed in Chapter 1, war is not a political act. Indeed, in his view **war** is a consequence of the political process actually having broken down. Carl von Clausewitz, the nineteenth-century Prussian strategist, however, highlighted the intricate link between war and politics. He argued war is 'a true political instrument, a continuation of political activity by other means' (Clausewitz 1976: 87). In other words, violence, or the threat of violence, in an anarchic international system can be a very effective manner for a state to secure its interests. Given this reality, and the prevalence of wars in world history, it is only natural that political scholars examine these conflicts in detail.

An obvious issue for IR students to tackle is why wars occur. After all, one of the main motivations of the whole discipline is to try and promote peaceful conflict resolution. In this respect, is it not possible to make war obsolete by studying the evidence and improving our understanding of such conflicts? The information gathered could then be utilised for finding solutions to this very human problem.

The causes of war seem to be numerous. At the broadest level, for instance, some scholars propose that human beings are naturally violent and conflict is thus inevitable, as evidenced by the frequency of wars fought throughout the ages. Others, however, argue that even if war has been a natural predication in the past, human nature can change. It is possible for political stability to be created by international institutions establishing an international rule of law. We will come back to this '**Realist**' versus '**Idealist**' debate later in the chapter. In the meantime, however, it is enough to point out that students of IR will be invited to engage in this 'nature' versus 'nurture' debate.

IR specialists have also identified more specific causes of war. These, for instance, include clashes over territory. This has traditionally been the most common spark of warfare. Classic examples of such actions include imperial powers expanding their empires (Russia and the Soviet Union regularly invading Poland, for instance), the desire for strategic territory (Israel's occupation of the Golan Heights in 1967), 'indigenous' forces freeing themselves from a colonial power (the War of Independence creating the USA, or Mozambique's victory against the Portuguese empire in the 1970s), and 'irredentist' wars, where one state seeks to be reunited with its 'rightful' territory currently occupied by a neighbour (the ongoing border dispute between India and Pakistan in Kashmir).

Along with territorial considerations, there are also economic motivations for war. Many clashes throughout history have been prompted by the protection of markets and trading routes. The competition for raw materials can also cause conflict. The Boer War at the beginning of the last century, for instance, was largely fought for control over South Africa's diamonds and gold. It could similarly be argued that Kuwait's oil supplies helped underwrite the West's interest in the Gulf War of 1991. Add to the territorial and economic motivations issues such as ideological clashes (World War II, with fascism versus **liberalism**, or the Cold War with **communism** versus capitalism), perceived self-defence (Israel again), ethnic rivalry (the Balkans in the twentieth century), war as a distraction (Argentina invading the Falklands/Malvinas in 1982 to deflect attention away from this Argentina's economic problems, and Britain's response, which had the same effect), and the overall causes of war start to mount up. And this is even before we consider civil wars (which also often have an international dimension) or acts of international terrorism where the violence is directed at symbols of the state or civilian targets. The study of war, in short, can tell us much about how states interact with each other, and indeed there is a whole sub-branch of IR, **Strategic Studies**, that specialises in how states deploy violence.

It would be wrong to think, however, that warfare is the dominant international relationship. It is **diplomacy** that wins this title. Indeed, there is usually room for some negotiation even during a war. As Thomas Schelling puts it, 'Pure conflict, in which the interests of the two antagonists are completely opposed, is a special case, it would arise in a war of complete extermination . . .' (Schelling 1980: 4). There is usually some common ground between states, even if this is only an agreement on how to treat prisoners of war or how to deal with civilians caught up in the fighting. Diplomacy can go to work even here.

Diplomacy is *the art of mitigating or reducing conflict, or promoting cooperation, by the means of persuasion or compromise.* Diplomats are thus employed to undertake two tasks. They identify common interests amongst states, paving a way for mutually beneficial actions (a trade agreement, perhaps, or even cooperation such as the European Union). Or, alternatively, they identify likely conflicts of interest and seek ways of minimising the consequences of such clashes (an arms reduction treaty, maybe, or a compromise linking issues together). In the name of these two objectives, diplomatic envoys and ambassadors have been exchanged between states since ancient times. The modern network of embassies, consulates and intergovernmental institutions across the world ensures that there are open channels of communication between most states. Diplomatic relations will usually even occur between obvious antagonists. The United States maintained an embassy in Moscow throughout the Cold War, for example, because even these two combatants had shared interests, most notably the avoidance of a nuclear war. In this respect, although it has to be remembered that power is the key to an anarchic international system, it remains a fact that most of the time it is diplomacy, not war, that determines the outcome of world politics.

Empirical case studies

Another topic essential to an apprenticeship in International Relations is **empirical case study**. Students of the sub-discipline should be aware of historical events illustrating how states have interacted in the past. These case studies help to show how the above theoretical notions, such as sovereignty, war and diplomacy, work themselves out in reality.

IR scholars have gone to great lengths to build a library of evidence that helps to explain how states react to their external environments. They have gathered examples from all areas of the globe and have likewise studied foreign relations throughout time. Whether it is the fall of the Roman empire, Napoleon's European adventurism at the turn of the nineteenth century, the origins of the First World War or the Palestinian campaign for nationhood in more contemporary times, each case study adds to the overall picture of how international relations work.

Two case studies that appear on the curricula of most university Politics programmes are the 'Cold War' and the 'New World Order'. The Cold War, between the United States and the Soviet Union, dominated global relations from the end of the Second World War until the late 1980s. It is a conflict that can be used to illustrate many key issues in IR. Students, for instance, can explore factors such as the dangers of ideological conflict, they can see how the mechanics of the **balance of power** actually work, they can judge the effectiveness of deterrents, and they can explore the consequences for 'peripheral states' when dominant powers are locked in stalemate. Similarly, case studies focusing on the New World Order also prove to be invaluable. Post-Cold War, where there is only one 'superpower', is theoretically a time in history when the United States can stamp its authority on the world. Indeed, there have been times when the West has ignored state sovereignty, intervening in territories to protect human **rights** and democratic ideals (Somalia, Bosnia and Kosovo). We have also seen the United States overthrow a sovereign government in Afghanistan, on the grounds that it was harbouring terrorists. Yet students on these New World Order courses should ask themselves why we now have *more* conflict in the world when compared to the Cold War years. And why has the United States not intervened more? It would seem, even post-Cold War, we are still very much living in an anarchical international system.

This is why case studies are so valuable. If we add the lessons learnt from analysing the Cold War and the New World Order to the evidence gathered from the other **modules** available on Politics programmes, then the overall picture of the mechanics of international relations becomes clearer. Empirical case studies build the platform from which generalised theories of state interaction can be constructed.

International organisations

So far, this chapter has been compatible with the traditional view of International Relations in that it has concentrated on the interaction between states. States, however, are not the only actors within the world system. International organisations also play a key role, and, as such, are important topics of study within the sub-discipline. International organisations can be categorised into three broad groups: intergovernmental organisations (IGOs), non-governmental organisations (NGOs), and transnational corporations (TNCs).

Intergovernmental organisations are formal institutions established to act as channels of conflict resolution, mediation, cooperation and problem-solving amongst states. As their name suggests, they are controlled and based around a nucleus of member states. They may be far ranging in their brief, such as the Commonwealth, consisting of Britain and its former colonies, or concentrate on a single issue, the International Atomic Energy Agency for example. Similarly, IGOs may consist of numerous member states, the United Nations with an almost universal membership, or be restricted to a specific group of countries, such as the Arab League representing the interests of Middle Eastern and North African states. IGOs are important within the international system as they provide regional stability (the African Union, the Organisation of American States and the European Union), economic assistance (the International Monetary Fund and **World Bank**), military deterrence or peacekeeping (the United Nations and the North Atlantic Treaty Organisation), health and social services (the World Health Organisation), and international regulation (the International Court of Justice).

It has to be remembered, however, that intergovernmental

organisations are only as effective as their member states let them be. They may indeed be good fora for conflict resolution and problem-solving, but it is an inherent reality of the international system that each individual member state will still try to promote its own *national* interest through these bodies. This has often led to a single state defying the decisions of the majority by vetoing a proposed action, or, alternatively, simply failing to comply with an IGO policy. Israel and South Africa, for instance, spent the whole of the Cold War period ignoring UN General Assembly resolutions calling upon them to negotiate with Palestinian leaders and representatives of the black majority in their respective territories. Given that there is no higher authority than the individual sovereign state in the world system, there is little that can be done, short of coercive measures, if states elect to reject IGO decisions.

Of all the major IGOs, only the European Union (EU) has gone a step further to address this issue. Here, the member states have formed a **supranational organisation**. This is to say, in some policy areas, the individual countries have given up their right to veto an EU decision. In effect, members have pooled their sovereignty, in an attempt to promote political stability and economic prosperity. As a result, the European Union becomes a higher authority, with EU law being superior to that of the national laws of the member states. This IGO is the closest that human beings have come to the ideal of regional or world government. The hesitancy of some EU members to take this experiment further is a clear indication of how reluctant individual states are to give up their sovereignty.

Along with IGOs, *non*-governmental organisations also influence international relations. Although NGOs are nominally independent of state power, many are respected within world politics because of their expertise, the opinion they represent, or the services they provide. Just as stable domestic political environments need organisations outside the state to assist with the smooth running of a society, so does the international system. Influential transnational **interest groups** have developed around such issues as religion (the World Council of Churches), the environment (Greenpeace), development aid (Oxfam), human rights (the Anti-Apartheid Movement), and sport (the International Olympic Committee). The scale of world opinion mobilised by such groups has forced states to listen to these particular NGOs. Elsewhere, the work of the Movement of the International Red Cross and Red Crescent is respected because of their activity in war zones, where it would be impossible for state agents to operate, while NGOs such as Amnesty International provide a useful function in bringing abusive governments to account. Groups like these are now very much part of the international system.

Perhaps the most influential of the non-state actors, however, are **transnational corporations**. As we have seen in the other chapters of this book, economics and politics are intricately linked, and this is just the same in the international environment. Even medium-sized businesses today can be found operating in multiple countries. Indeed, in many Third World cases we find TNCs enjoying financial turnovers much larger than the annual budgets of their host governments. With so much money at stake, and the inequality that accompanies this, questions of influence and exploitation are bound to arise. TNCs are thus very much political actors. There can be little doubt, for example, that the lobbying by Western companies successfully delayed sanctions being placed on South Africa, despite this government's prolonged abuse of human rights under apartheid. Similarly, China's recent indiscretions have been treated leniently by Western governments because of the vast economic potential this market offers to TNCs. Business lobbying, in the same manner, also persuaded George W. Bush to abandon US commitments to the 1997 Kyoto Protocols on the environment. These examples would suggest that any scholar seeking to understand international relations should also look beyond the state, taking into account the activities of non-state actors, TNCs included.

International Political Economy

Given this link between economics and politics, it is only
natural that a specific specialist field of **International Political
Economy** (IPE) has developed within IR. So, alongside understanding the nature of the international system, how international relations are conducted, case studies and international
organisations, all students of the sub-discipline should also
have at least a working knowledge of IPE. Assisting this, some
of the most interesting modules available in British universities
concentrate on the more radical side of IPE.

Indeed, as it will be discussed later in the chapter, Marxists
regard economics to be the key determinate of world events.
They, for example, explain the great European colonialism of
the nineteenth and twentieth centuries in terms of states
seeking raw materials and overseas markets. Similarly, others
blame the current inequality between the First and Third
Worlds on a systematic **underdevelopment** of the poorer
states. These theorists argue that Western wealth simply could
not have been generated without the exploitation of the
peripheral economies of South America, Asia and Africa
(see Frank 1969, for example). Even if one is not convinced
by this underdevelopment thesis, it is hard to deny that,
historically, Western governments have called the shots economically. In the last two decades of the twentieth century, for
instance, the poorer countries have been forced to adopt neo-
liberal policies (free trade and minimum state intervention) if
they were to continue to receive essential development aid. In
this respect, Western states are effectively making policy
decisions on behalf of other societies, a notional respect for
state sovereignty not withstanding. These are just some of the
issues that students of IPE can get their teeth into during their
university studies.

An investigation of IPE is thus recommended. It is pathway
into many fascinating debates, and a method of comprehend-
ing many of the most pressing issues relating to wealth and
inequality that permeate international relations today. Indeed,
if IPE is studied along with the other four topics highlighted in

this section, then your overall understanding of the sub-discipline will develop well.

THE DIFFERENT THEORETICAL APPROACHES WITHIN INTERNATIONAL RELATIONS

International Relations is not just about studying international history, despite this providing invaluable empirical evidence. Nor is IR solely about following current world affairs, although this should be done diligently. Instead, the key to International Relations is using the empirical evidence from these two sources to construct theories. In this respect, we have already seen how scholars use concepts such as *sovereignty* and *underdevelopment* to assist their understanding. Beyond these concepts, however, whole schools of thought have developed. This is where the empirical evidence and the individual concepts are drawn together to create much larger, overarching theories of how international politics work.

As with all the social sciences, however, IR scholars have failed to come up with a single commonly recognised theory of International Relations. Indeed, considerable disagreement has led to several theoretical schools forming. This section will introduce the most popular amongst these schools, as by exploring these different approaches more can be learnt about the nature of International Relations itself. It will be up to the individual reader, however, to decide for themselves which of these schools, or which combination of these theories, they find the most convincing.

The Realists

Jean-Jacques Rousseau, the political philosopher, wrote back in the eighteenth century that 'the tragedy of international society is that it is in everyone's social interest to have a commonly agreed sovereign power, but it is in the interests of each individual state to flout that authority when it is to its advantage' (cited in Anderson 1996: 200). This, for many, is the reality of international relations. These people have a conservative view of the world, based upon the assumption that states will always seek to further their own interests, and, importantly, this will often occur at the expense of fellow members within the world system. In their opinion, states are rational actors that will consistently look after themselves in the first instance, and thus cannot necessarily be trusted to cooperate.

These **Realist** scholars point to the anarchic nature of the international system. As it lacks Rousseau's 'commonly agreed sovereign power', we are, once again, in Hobbes' 'state of nature'. In this respect, without the protection of the rule of law or a world government, the key to survival and influence within this system is self-reliance and power. This is why realists believe that it is the first duty of the state in the international arena to maximise its power in relation to the other states, power being the only commodity that can guarantee security and prosperity. It is a world of dog eat dog, and not much can be done about this.

Many Realists therefore regard the international system as amoral (though not immoral). Laws and **justice** are more suited to the domestic arena. A state's primary obligation in the international setting is its own security and to further its own national interest. Any deviation from this self-reliant path risks displaying weakness. As Kenneth Waltz puts it, 'Nationally, the force of a government is exercised in the name of right and justice. Internationally, the force of a state is employed for the sake of its own protection and advantage' (Waltz 1979: 112).

It has been this Realist approach that has dominated both in the study and practice of International Relations throughout history. Thucydides (1954) identified aspects of Realism in the Peloponnesian Wars of ancient Greece, just as the Cold War warriors followed similar realist strategies much later, in the second half of the twentieth century. The key to this Realist world is the balance of power. If the first objective of a state is to promote its own interests, attempting to increase its share of international power, this is rarely achieved through an over-aggressive foreign policy. Most often it will be more beneficial to maintain the *staus quo*, ensuring a balance of power between all the major players within the system. The 'great powers' of Europe, for example, were relatively successful in achieving equilibrium in the hundred years following the 1815 Battle of Waterloo. They acted as a 'concert of nations', holding regular diplomatic summits to ensure that no one state gained an advantage that could result in instability.

Similarly, a balance of power was maintained throughout the Cold War with Europe being divided between Western and Eastern blocks. Both Moscow and Washington had their own spheres of influence. If the United States felt the Soviets were gaining an advantage somewhere in the periphery, however, then resources would be committed to neutralise this influence. In some cases, this resulted in Washington aiding authoritarian dictatorships such as the Somoza dynasty in Nicaragua (until their overthrow in 1979) or Marcos in the Philippines (1966 to 1986). Yet the amoral nature of realist foreign policy dictated that this was entirely justifiable, as the primary interest of the United States had to be the containment of communism and the protection of its own national interest. Relative peace was thus achieved through a mindset of mutual mistrust, with both states constantly working to maintain a balance of power, immediately adjusting its policy should its competitor seek to gain an advantage. This, it was argued, was the only 'realistic' way to deal with an anarchic international system of competing states.

The Idealists

Not all scholars, however, agree with this Realist approach to international relations. Many so-called **Idealists** feel that states should concentrate more on the actual causes of conflict, rather than just managing the consequences of power imbalances. After the devastation of the First World War, for example, where the hundred-year 'concert of nations' balance of power broke down with catastrophic results, there was a considerable effort to establish international institutions that could promote conflict resolution and mediation. These bodies could be utilised as an alternative to war. In effect, politicians were attempting to establish Rousseau's superior 'commonly agreed sovereign power' in the international setting.

Those who backed this new League of Nations argued that if states could manufacture peace and stability in their own domestic societies, via enforcing a rule of law and establishing government, why could this not be done internationally? Would not international laws policed by international institutions bring an end to inter-state violence? Similarly, could not peace be maintained by 'collective security' where states pledge to intervene against an aggressor should one of their number be attacked? Indeed, if the richer states acted more to reduce inequality in the world, this would also contribute to an international system less prone to violence. So, instead of following the realists and trying to work within the existing distrustful arena of competing sovereign states, Idealists aim to build an **international society** where it would benefit all to respect basic international laws and norms.

To a limited extent, the Idealists' goals have been met. Although the League of Nations failed to stop World War II, its successor, the United Nations, has become a respected international authority. Also, there is today an increased recognition of international law amongst individual states. Most wars, for example, are fought within the stipulations of the Geneva Convention, while the International Court of Justice has been successful in resolving a number of inter-state disputes without recourse to violence. There have even been several beneficial international peacekeeping operations, and, with the Gulf War of 1991, an act of collective security.

Yet, despite these successes, states still remain reluctant to give up their sovereignty. Instances of vetoing or ignoring the decisions of international institutions remain common, while, at the same time, member states are often unwilling to commit their own national resources to funding or arming these international bodies. Consequently, inter-state conflict is still a prominent feature of world politics. In this respect, it is safe to conclude that Idealist views may have helped create a less anarchic international system in modern times, but we are still a long way off from establishing a world government or a functioning international society. This conclusion, however, does not mean that it is impossible to reach these goals.

The radicals

Alongside the Realists and the Idealists is the **radical school** of International Relations. These scholars point to the elite nature of foreign policy. Given that so few individuals determine the direction of a state's external actions, it has to be questioned whom this foreign policy establishment actually represents. Marxists, for example, would argue that these elites do not promote their country's collective *national* interests, but instead they represent narrower *class* interests. Just as these theorists consider that the domestic government is merely an executive committee acting on behalf of the bourgeoisie, it follows that foreign policy decision-makers also project this same bourgeois interest into the external environment. Consequently, Marxists contend that international relations are dominated by capitalist competition. Each national group is seeking to control access to raw materials, production resources and markets across the world. They also insure that a system of world trade is maintained where the West can prosper at the expense of the Third World. The rhetoric used by foreign policy decision-makers may talk about the national interest and the spread of liberal democracy, but in reality only elite interests are being served. The working class thus gains little from international relations, despite it being this class that sacrifices most when it comes to fighting wars.

This school of thought may now seem outdated, especially given the collapse of the Soviet Union and decolonisation in the Third World. Yet IR scholars would be unwise to dismiss all the ideas presented by the radical school. After all, the remaining massive inequality between the First and Third

Worlds has still to be accounted for, as do the reasons for transnational corporations seeming to have so much influence within foreign policy circles. Could it indeed be true that certain classes are represented more than others through the conduct of international relations?

Feminist theory

According to feminists, it is not only the working class that is excluded from foreign policy decision-making. Women are also under-represented within this elite. Just as women have found it difficult to get their voices heard in domestic politics, they have also been disenfranchised when it comes to international relations. Male-dominated institutions have ensured that if the interests of women have been expressed, this has largely been done by men. Women have had little opportunity to represent themselves, and will not be able to do so until discrimination is fully removed from these institutions.

Some feminist theorists take this notion of disenfranchisement further. They argue that, since women are largely excluded form the external arena, this actually effects the nature of international relations. They portray the destructive forces of world politics – competition, aggression and war – as being typically male characteristics. If women were also at the helm, it follows, maybe their more nurturing and peace-loving nature would make for a better world.

The actions of women who have reached high office, however, would seem to contradict this claim. If we look at leaders such as Margaret Thatcher, Indira Ghandi, Madeline Albright or Jeane Kirkpatrick, these women have displayed hawkish tendencies as keen as their male counterparts. It therefore seems unlikely that international relations, or domestic politics for that matter, can be accurately explained by simply assigning 'typical' characteristics to the respective genders. This reductionism is at the expense of all the other variables, mentioned above, that influence international relations. However, until women do gain equal access to this external environment, these feminist ideas remain a difficult school of thought to dismiss.

The institutional focus

Another methodological approach used to study IR involves an 'institutional focus'. Getting away from the ideological schools above, these scholars seek to analyse international relations by identifying how decisions are actually made. They portray foreign policy as being the product of a bureaucratic process rather that merely ideological desires. As Graham Allison puts it, 'To explain why a particular formal govern-mental decision was made, or why one pattern of government behaviour emerged, it is necessary to identify the games and players, to display the coalitions, bargains, and compromises, and to convey some feel for the confusion' (Allison 1971: 146). To use the analogy of chess, international politics is not just a case of two leaders single-handedly weighing up their options and then moving their pieces accordingly. The leader may have the overall authority to make the moves, but, given the complexity of the game, he or she has to rely on many others to supply accurate intelligence and strategy options. Indeed, it may even be the case that several lesser actors are responsible for moving some of the pieces independently. The final foreign policy will only be achieved after a complex series of decisions involving many individuals and several agencies within the government concerned.

The policy process itself, therefore, has a major impact on the policy outcome. Why, for example, did country A decide to build and deploy a new fleet of ships as a deterrent against country B? Certainly, all within A's government agree that country B should be contained. Yet it may have been that the naval option was taken because the navy possessed better bureaucratic infighting skills than the airforce, and thus con-vinced the leader to back their preferred option. Ships were therefore deployed rather than aircraft. Foreign policy bureau-cracies, in this respect, are not monolithic. They invariably host competing **factions** with different opinions and interests. External policies will reflect the outcome of this bureaucratic competition. This is why the student of IR has to be aware of how a decision was made just as much as what this decision was. Only if both of these facts are known will a full understanding of why a particular policy was implemented become clear.

SUMMARY

International Relations, then, is the sub-discipline of Politics that concentrates on the external arena. This, by and large, involves a focus on relations between, and amongst, states. Such a focus, however, should not rule out the work of non-state actors. For, as we have seen, NGOs and TNCs also have a considerable role to play in the politics of the external environment.

Students who choose to study this field will be exposed to a number of concepts in order to develop their knowledge of foreign relations. They will learn to understand, amongst other issues, the nature of the international system, including the value of 'state sovereignty'. They will explore how external relations are conducted through war and diplomacy. They will be introduced to international organisations, and they will link the political to the economic in terms of investigating IPE. All this will be assisted by case studies, gathering empirical evidence from across the world and throughout time. By the end of their degree, students will have no problem in deploying these abstract concepts in order to explain the unravelling events in the international system around them.

Also assisting students to develop an overall understanding of the sub-discipline are the theoretical schools of IR (led by Realism, Idealism, **feminism**, insitutionalism, and the radical approach). These schools gather together the individual concepts in order to build an overarching approach to the subject. Students are free to follow any one of these theoretical paths, they may choose another, or mix and match. What will be required, however, is that, as scholars of IR, students should combine the empirical and the theoretical to build a firm notion of how the external political environment actually works. From this position they can then go on to make judgements about the current international system, and whether it is managed correctly.

FURTHER READING

For those readers who want to learn more about International Relations, a good place to start is two excellent textbooks by Nicholson (2002) and Russett et al. (2000). They both provide comprehensive and accessible overviews of this sub-discipline. If, however, you want to concentrate more on the individual issues raised in this chapter, Berridge (2002) can be read on diplomacy, Buzan (1987) on war and security, and Gilpin (2001) on International Political Economy. In terms of the approaches to IR, Morgenthau (1985) is the seminal source on Realism, Bull (2002) puts forward the Idealist case, Rosenberg (1994) captures many of the views advocated by the radicals, whilst Enloe (1992) outlines the feminist perspective of International Relations. Two other books worth mentioning, that offer both empirical case studies and examples of how the 'foreign policy analysis' method works, are Allison (1971) on the Cuban missile crisis and, at the risk of pushing my own work, Thomson (1996) on the conundrum of US policy towards apartheid South Africa.

PART III
Politics and Study Skills

Ken Phillips

7 SKILLS FOR STUDYING POLITICS

Learning outcomes for study skills

On completion of this chapter, you should have learned about the following:

1. Key aspects of learning and assessment in the study of Politics

2. The importance of taking a strategic approach to your learning and assessment

3. The range of resources for learning about Politics

4. The range of assessments used in Politics and approaches to them

5. Being reflective about your learning and assessment.

Welcome to this chapter. This chapter and the one that follows are not an afterthought, tagged on to the 'real' part of the book. These chapters are here to help you to get the most out of your time studying Politics. The basic starting point of this chapter is the view that *all* students need guidance on how to study at university and that this is the time for trying out new ways of learning. It is designed to help you to respond to the different challenges that *higher* education presents.

Learning effectively is a very complex skill, and no apology is given for using the word *skill* in both this chapter and the next. This chapter considers the skills you need to study

Politics successfully, while Chapter 8 deals with how the skills you have gained as a student of Politics are transferable to the world beyond the university.

So please read on and get a feel for what is covered in this chapter, and use it as a resource to come back to as you proceed through your studies. It is not really designed to be read from beginning to end, but rather to be dipped into as and when it is relevant.

I have tried to make the content as relevant as possible to Politics. The box on page 131 lists the outcomes I hope you will have learned after using this chapter.

CENTRAL FEATURES IN LEARNING AND ASSESSMENT IN POLITICS

Teaching and assessment in Politics shares many features with the other subjects in the social sciences and humanities and indeed you may well be studying one of these as well. Before considering these more general features, students of Politics should give particular attention in their learning and assessments to the following more distinctive factors:

1. Conceptualisation
2. Comparison
3. Theory and competing perspectives
4. Importance of primary sources

As we have seen in earlier chapters, much of the subject matter of Politics is *conceptual*. By this we mean that it is about ideas rather than concrete realities. Indeed, as Chapter 1 highlighted, one of the most fiercely disputed concepts in the discipline is that of 'politics' itself and many undergraduate programmes devote some time to the age-old question of 'what is politics?'. Students are expected to have knowledge, for example, of the basic facts of how politics and government works, how many members sit in legislative assemblies, the powers of the executive and how votes are cast and counted.

More importantly they should know how and where to find out such factual knowledge. Crucially, they also need to understand that concepts like *legislation*, *the executive* and *voting* are ideas that are socially constructed and which need to be defined and understood.

The subject of Politics abounds with concepts like these, and other even more central ones like *power*, *authority* and *influence*. There are no universal definitions and the meanings of them are still heavily contested. Understanding and using these concepts is not made easier by the fact that many of them are part of everyday language. As students of Politics it is important to build up your conceptual vocabulary and make clear in discussions and writing the meanings you attach to them (Renwick and Swinburn 1987).

All higher education students are expected to be 'analytical'. By this I mean not just being able to describe something but to consider the why, when and how questions.

One of the major strategies by which the study of Politics is made analytical is through *comparison*. Much of the excitement in studying Politics comes from the vast variation that exists in political institutions and behaviours. Communities and societies through the ages and around the globe at the present time have all found different ways to bring a sense of order to their collective affairs. This variety provides a rich vein of inquiry for comparative political analysis to explain why and how these differences exist. Even if we only want to understand the politics and government of our own county, it does not take long to realise that a key to this understanding is to examine how it differs from either earlier times or other countries. If nothing else, such comparisons help us to realise that there are alternatives and hence choices in the way we are governed. As a Politics student, you should therefore look for ways to demonstrate evidence of drawing on comparisons.

We are all familiar with the phrase 'theory and practice' and in our everyday lives we are happy to criticise something as 'ok in theory but not really workable in practice', or some such phrase. For example, in cricket we might be instructed in the theory of how to stand at the wicket and hit the ball but find that this is not always easy to put into practice. When we try and apply this phrase to academic study, students invariably find the transition from everyday usage difficult. Theory applied to concepts seems to raise fears that don't apply to more everyday activities: theories of **democracy** or political **obligation,** for example, seem to be much more daunting than those on playing cricket or baking a cake!

Part of the solution is to demystify the academic use of the term 'theory' and to recognise it simply refers to attempts to make statements of general validity about something. Another is to distinguish between normative and empirical theories, both of which are present in the study of Politics. By **normative theory** I mean generalised statements on how political affairs *ought* to operate and this is largely the concern of political thought. Thus, for example, Hobbes was writing in *Leviathan* way back in 1651 about how he felt government *should* be regarded and organised if mankind was to progress from the horrors of the natural order as he saw it. At the more 'scientific' end of the spectrum, empirical theory is an attempt to find generalised statements on how politics actually operates in practice (the 'is' rather than the 'ought'). Such theory is important because it helps us to move from a narrow to a broad level of understanding. Using the language of theory, we say that theory should contain hypotheses or propositions against which we can research practice to find out if the theory is valid or whether it needs amending or replacing. These theories might be wide ranging and universalistic in their coverage of Politics – and good examples of these would be Marxist, pluralist, functional or elitist theories – or relatively narrow and particular, like theories of *coups d'état* or election systems.

Exercise

Try to think of a broad explanation (theory) of why there is a difference in voting between men and women. What hypotheses does your theory lead to and how would you go about testing them?

Given the variety of political arrangements, and the fact that we are concerned with the behaviour of human beings who are capable of independent action, it is not surprising that there are few if any proven and widely accepted theories about Politics. (If there were we could call them laws of politics. Have you heard of the 'Iron Law of Oligarchy' that states that all organisations over time will end up being controlled by a few people?) Thus another distinctive feature of studying Politics is the need to be aware of *competing theories* (or we could call them 'perspectives', if the word theory remains a stumbling block). As students of Politics, therefore, you should work towards identifying and comparing different explanations/theories/perspectives and assessing their relative strengths and weaknesses when measured against 'the facts'. You will be amazed at how much credit you will get from your tutors if you are able to do this!

The final feature that is a strong component of studying Politics is the need, whenever possible, to draw on *primary sources*. By primary sources I mean largely written documents that form the main base of evidence about politics rather than interpretations of the evidence provided by academic writers, researchers and political commentators. In political thought and philosophy, these primary sources are the original works of the theorists and philosophers. In respect of political systems and government they might take the form of formal documents like **constitutions** and government legislation and reports or even the raw (unworked) data of political surveys. It is good practice to go back, wherever possible, to these primary sources rather than always rely on the coverage of them by others. Indeed, it is surprising how often the original primary source is easier to understand than someone else's interpretation of it.

Learning strategically

Learning is at the heart of education and by this I mean something very different to being taught. You will hopefully learn about politics from your teachers (who like to be distinguished from their counterparts in schools by being called lecturers) but you will also learn from your fellow students and from your own independent studies and perhaps also from your own observation of the political world. What makes learning at university distinctive is that it is informed by the latest scholarship and research and above all that it is informed by a critical perspective, constantly questioning existing knowledge and ideas.

Learning is one of the most demanding and fulfilling aspects of human existence and this is particularly the case in respect of learning about politics. Politics, as we have seen, is concerned with one of the most important aspects of human activity and it has been studied as far back as records go. It has an immensely rich and wide-ranging literature that increasingly takes on a daunting prospect for study as its quantity has exploded as a result of the current revolution in information. I shall be outlining some of these sources later, but it is important to emphasise first the benefits of a *strategic* approach to learning to deal with the wealth of learning opportunities that you will have on your course.

To help with this, I am going to give you some general guiding principles on learning about Politics and encourage you to find out what works best for your learning style:

1. Setting your goals and objectives
2. Organising your learning
3. Learning actively and deeply
4. Learning independently

1. Setting your goals and objectives
Students of Politics are special and often differ from their fellow students studying other subjects. Despite its universality and importance, politics suffers from a bad image. How often have we heard the phrase 'the world/county/town/community would be a better place without all this politics'? So as a student of Politics you have already risen above this common prejudice. Many of you may also be inspired by the potential

to become involved in politics at either the national, local or group level. And implicitly (if not explicitly) you have demonstrated that you are not afraid to examine and analyse conflict.

To be successful as a student (and indeed as an actual or potential activist) the overriding imperative is to be clear and articulate about your learning goals and objectives as these will help you to remain motivated when you are faced with the inevitable crises that contemporary university students experience.

Exercise on deciding your reasons for studying Politics

Write down your responses to the following questions and review them periodically during your course:

Why did I choose to study Politics?
What aspects of Politics do I want to specialise in?
How well do I want to do in terms of assessment grades?
What do I hope to do after graduating?
Is the subject of Politics helpful/relevant to my longer-term life goals?

The above questions will help you to clarify your longer-term goals but you will also need to break these down into shorter-term and more task-specific objectives. The latter can be related to the principle of organised learning.

2. Organising your learning
There is some truth in the adage that being successful in higher education is down to motivation (40 per cent), organisation (40 per cent) and ability (20 per cent). Organising your learning is particularly important for today's students who have so many other competing demands on their study time, and increasingly the need to earn money. Organised learning requires you to have a system for collecting and storing information (discussed later) and the ability to manage your time.

One of the first tasks presented to you when you start your course will be to construct your timetable of classes and this needs to become the fulcrum around which you attempt to manage your broader learning time. You will need to build into your class timetable periods for preparing for lectures, and especially seminars and tutorials, and for reflecting on what you have learnt in classes. The other axis for managing your time should be your assessment calendar. Most tutors now give information at the beginning of their courses/**modules** on how you will be assessed together with deadlines for submissions. As more and more universities adopt the two-semester year this will inevitably tend towards a bunching of coursework assessment dates into the third quarter of the semester. Your objective should be to spread your assessment preparation work over the two middle quarters of the semester – ensuring that you have gained a clear insight into what is required of you in the first quarter, and leaving the final quarter of the semester to preparing for examinations or end-of-module tests. If you build in time for preparing assessments into your weekly timetable you will then be able to individualise this for each week with the specific tasks and goals you need to set yourself. Ideally, you should also be clear on the priority order of these goals and tasks. In thinking about priorities try and remember that what is the most important is not always the most urgent. And try to be disciplined about putting your least favoured tasks higher in the list and thus avoid the temptation to leave them to another time – they are probably the tasks you need to work hardest at, but once out of the way the rest of your week will get better!

Exercise on organising your learning

If you have access to a computer, experiment with one of the many diary management software programmes and devise a method for recording your semester timetable to include recurring times for classes and blocks of time for reading and assessment preparation. Think how you might individualise each weekly timetable by including specific goals and tasks to be achieved and how you can show their relative priority.

You will find more guidance on time management in the next chapter.

3. Learning actively and deeply

There is a vast body of literature from psychologist and educationalists on how we learn. What comes through consistently is that learning is most effective when we are actively (rather than passively) engaged in the process. The passive learner considers studying as little more than recording and regurgitating the 'facts' as presented by tutors and in the literature. The active learner, in contrast, is constantly using the information gathered to seek out ways of making connections and attempting to reformulate it, as she or he understands it.

Looking for connections when studying will result in deep rather than surface learning.

The notion of 'depth' is central to what distinguishes study at the university level. In some ways this is another way of saying that in higher education we attempt to explain why, what, and how things are the way they are. Why does Britain have a simple majority electoral system? What impact does this have on the way politics operates? How might it be different? Nothing is taken for granted: everything needs an explanation. But from a learning perspective, depth is also about us personalising what we are learning through thought and reflection. In short, this is all about engaging our brains rather than expecting the brain to passively sponge up the information it is receiving. Over the centuries, many of the most gifted in terms of brainpower have written and thought about politics. As a student of Politics, you are fortunate to have the opportunity to look at the work of some of them, but also to be engaged, like they were, in attempting to think about and explain some of the most fundamental questions about the nature of the human condition.

Exercise on learning actively

When studying a source on a particular topic (say, a journal article on political parties), consider some of the following questions:

1. How does what I am studying compare with how the topic was presented in the lecture?

2. What is this source adding to my knowledge?

3. Does the source define key concepts differently from others?

4. Is there one main point that makes this source's contribution distinctive?

5. What links are there between this topic and other topics I have studied, including other subjects I am studying?

6. Are there any competing perspectives being put forward?

7. What are the primary sources of evidence in the reading (research findings, government publications, original texts, etc.)?

---

4. Learning independently

Earlier in the chapter I said that studying Politics at university is about learning rather than being taught. More accurately I should have said learning independently. Although you can expect committed support from your tutors, you need to recognise that you are responsible for your learning. Hence the emphasis above on the learning principles of identifying your goals and objects, organising your work, managing your time, and taking an active approach to your learning. Further guidance on self-directed learning from books and articles is given later.

Learning independently does not necessarily mean learning in isolation from others. Learning is best achieved as a social process in which you are working and communicating with others, the most important of whom are your fellow students. This is most obviously achieved in seminars but can just as importantly take place, for example, over a coffee in the refectory. Maybe we should think in terms of interdependent learning and this is explored more fully in the next chapter.

Suggestion

Why not get together with some like-minded students and form a study group, meeting socially to discuss your studies and to share advice and information?

Your learning style

Your reactions to the advice offered in the last section will probably depend upon the learning style you are most comfortable with. It is an obvious point, but we all learn differently. There is a vast literature on this topic, much of which attempts to categorise different types of learners and suggests that these are determined genetically or by other forces beyond our control. Of all the writers on learning styles, Kolb is still regarded by most as the guru (Kolb 1984, see also Pask 1978, and Honey and Mumford 1992). Kolb distinguishes four different 'ideal types' of learning styles based on alternative individual characteristics of brain functioning and personality.

Look at the exercise on page 142. Maybe you do not neatly fit any one category, or think it depends how you feel on a particular day or on what you are studying. You don't have to have a leaning towards any particular learning style to be a successful student of Politics – each has its own strengths and weaknesses. But you might like to consider the view that the aspects I have italicised above are particularly helpful for this subject. You need to consider developing these aspects in your own learning, if they have not been a feature before.

Exercise on Kolb's learning styles

Which of the following learning styles apply to you?

Accommodator: more interested in practice than theory, *enjoy working with others*, need variety and change, not good at planning and working out what you are going to write in advance.
Diverger: more *interested in learning from reflecting* on experience, can reflect on information and *see new ways of putting ideas and information together*, rather uncritical of other peoples ideas.
Converger: *enjoy problem-solving and gaining new skills, prefer to plan* well in advance, want to have a clear answer to questions, and work best as an individual rather than a group member.
Assimilator: more of an abstract thinker, *feel comfortable with theorising, good at organising ideas and linking them together,* want to know everything before ready to come to a conclusion.

Resources for learning about Politics

One thing is certain, as a student of Politics you will not be short of sources from which to learn. The following section offers brief accounts of the wide variety of such sources:

1. Lectures
2. Seminars and tutorials
3. The printed word
4. Computing and IT

and concludes with some guidance on how to consolidate your learning through remembering and recording information.

1. Learning from lectures

Putting lectures at the head of this list is not meant to indicate that they are the most important source of learning but they are what most of us associate with being a university student. Hopefully your experience of lectures will depart from the traditional image of the learned professor speaking to a host of passive students desperately trying to take down her or his every word. Lecturers these days are offered training in how to lecture and they are encouraged to be clear about what they expect their students to learn, to offer a diversity of learning experiences, and to adjust the pace and content to the attention span of their audience. Whether or not this is the case, we all know a good lecture is one that inspires students to continue discussing and reading more widely on the topic under consideration.

So what should you be seeking to learn from a lecture? It is certainly not a case of finding out all you need to know about a topic on the syllabus. Our view of what you should be taking from a Politics lecture is summed up in the following exercise.

Exercise on recording a lecture

Devise a pro forma or lecture note outline (preferably by word-processing) to include the following headings. Try it out in Politics lectures and constantly refine it:

1. Module code and title

2. Date of lecture

3. Name of lecturer

4. Topic

5. Key concepts and their authors

6. Key theories/perspectives/arguments and their contrasting strengths and weaknesses

7. Links with other topics/subjects

8. Five important 'facts'

9. Useful sources for reference

10. Points for further thought and/or consideration

11. Queries to take up at related seminars and tutorials

Hint: This should be no more than a maximum two sides of A4 paper, otherwise you will be tempted to write down too much and lose the main thread of the lecture as a result.

2. Learning from seminars and tutorials

Seminars should be very different from lectures, not just because there will be fewer students, but because in seminars the main source of learning should be from yourself and your fellow students. Yes, you can learn from yourself! If the seminar takes the form of a student presentation then you will find that your learning will be at its deepest when it is your turn to deliver the paper. We may think we understand something but the real test is whether we can convey that understanding to others and be able to respond to their questions. Its deep learning because it is 'double' learning – absorbing ideas and information and then conveying it back to others, meaningfully and coherently in real time.

How effective seminar learning is depends as much on the students as it does on the tutor. The tutor is responsible for devising an interesting programme of work for seminars, for keeping order and stopping the class straying too far from the point. But students have a responsibility to participate and to offer their thoughts, observations and questions to the discussion. And this means preparing beforehand.

Seminars should therefore be an opportunity to learn by articulating and trying out ideas and trains of thought, getting ideas and information from other students, and for testing the old adage that two (or more brains) are better than one. At their best, seminars are creative workshops of the mind! And from a politics perspective, they should be examples of democracy in practice, that is, based on freedom of speech, respect for the **rights** of others, and debating the extent of consensus and disagreement on the issue under consideration.

Tutorials are occasions when you will have the opportunity to meet with your tutors on a one-to-one or small group basis. You should use these opportunities to seek help and guidance with your studies, and even with personal issues that are affecting your work. In the case of the latter, the tutor can advise you on more specialist support that is available, if necessary. One way of making the best of these opportunities is to go along with a list of topics and questions that you want to go over with your tutor.

3. *Learning from the printed word*
More books and articles are written about politics than any other subject. Not all of these are written for an academic audience but they all present invaluable learning resources. The most obvious of these are *academic books and journal articles* for which your university library will be the main provider.

The vast majority of libraries organise their learning resources using the Dewey Decimal Classification and for political studies the main numbers are as follows: 320 to 329 for the main stock on governments and the political process, 341 for international political organisations, 350 to 355 on administration, American government, the military and war, and the 940s for political biographies. If you know the Dewey classification for the topic you are interested in you can search for resources on your own, thus demonstrating your ability to be an independent learner.

Card indexes are rapidly disappearing from university libraries and you will need to get skilled in using your library's computer-based catalogue. These are invaluable, but they do not totally replace the benefits to be gained from browsing the open shelves in the relevant section of the library. You will also need to get to know the arrangement your library has for holding and issuing short-term loan collections. These consist of books identified by your tutors as likely to be in most demand. If the book you are looking for is not in stock, reserve it, but don't give up. Go to the library shelves and see what alternative sources you can find for yourself. You should also have access to inter-library loans, but this may be on a restricted basis.

If you have problems, ask a member of the library staff for help.

Library exercise

Find out the Dewey classification for pressure groups and then work out how books are subdivided further within this classification. What, for example, is the Dewey classification for French pressure groups? Using your university's online catalogue, print off a list of books available in the library for your next seminar topic.

Academic books can be broadly divided up into textbooks (designed primarily for a student audience), monographs (containing write-ups of research or new thoughts), or major works (which are recognised as making an authoritative contribution to knowledge). Journal articles are primarily of the monograph type but have the advantage (hopefully) of being more up to date as the leadtime for publishing a book is much longer. Unlike books, relevant journal articles are much more difficult to track down. For the latter purpose there are the annual indexes of the journals but also collective indexes and abstracts (short summaries of the content of the articles). The main guide to journal articles on politics is the *International Political Science Abstract*.

In addition to the above, *dictionaries and encyclopaedias* offer a further library-based resource for learning. Bearing in mind the need to provide definitions of concepts in Politics, students are often tempted to quote from a mainstream dictionary. The problem is that such dictionaries are primarily about everyday rather than technical or academic usage of words. Better are the specialised dictionaries of Politics that have been compiled.

Examples of dictionaries of Politics

Laqueur, W. *Dictionary of Politics*
Roberts, G. K. *Dictionary of Political Analysis*
Robertson, D. *Penguin Dictionary of Politics*

Encyclopaedias are tempting sources as well, especially as versions on CD-ROM are now found in many homes. They are invariably written, however, with an emphasis on 'facts' and are, therefore, likely to be of limited value to the Politics student who is looking for competing theories and interpretations.

Newspapers and the political weeklies are an invaluable learning resource for students of Politics. As well as keeping you up to date with political news, the quality newspapers also include frequent feature articles analysing the political background to the news. As a student, you will be able to take reduced subscriptions to a quality newspaper, and getting into the habit of keeping a cuttings file is a good way of demonstrating your awareness of current developments. The same applies to the political weeklies, but for these – and indeed for newspapers as well – you need to be aware of their political leaning. The latter issue is one reason why you will need to have a critical perspective on what you read from these sources.

Your lecturers will recommend reading as a follow-up to lectures, in preparation for seminars, and to undertake assessed work. You will get the most out of the reading for lectures and seminars if they keep pace with each other. Sometimes, a lecture course will follow a set textbook but there will almost certainly be additional reading so that you can broaden your knowledge of the subject and assess different points of view.

Only once you have done the recommended reading should you start looking for additional reading. The set books might make recommendations, or you could browse the library shelves, or you could do a search on the library online catalogue. Subject searches are not always reliable. Sometimes keywords in the title can produce better results. This might produce such a wealth of material that you don't know where to start. A good guide is the number of times a book or article is cited in other people's bibliographies. You will see from this which texts are important reading. If you need help, ask your tutor.

When you are browsing, use the contents page or abstract to identify useful and interesting bits and scan to find the bits you want. Do not start at the beginning and try to work your way through; first make sure that the book or article has something to offer.

If you want to photocopy anything, you must obey the regulations on copyright displayed beside university photo-copying machines.

4. Learning from computing and information technology

We have all heard about the revolution resulting from the application of information technology and this applies in particular to its impact on political information and communications. *CD-ROMs* that store information for us to access on the computer are now commonplace and there are numerous examples that are very relevant to the study of Politics, for example, databases of newspaper articles, parliamentary proceedings, and indexes of books and journal articles. Increasingly, though, these are overshadowed by the *Internet* that allows us, through a *World Wide Web* browser (like Internet Explorer), to access information kept on computers around the world. You should be offered guidance on how to make the best use of this vast resource, including guidance on specific Internet sites that are useful for particular topics or good jumping-off points for your own information searches. The latter are more useful than using one of the various search engines that attempt to keep a universal database of web pages. This guidance should also cover the many 'health warnings' that you need to be aware of, including how to form judgements on the validity of the information provided and to cope with the temporary nature of many sites. These warnings even apply to the many 'official' sites of governments and governmental organisations around the world as well as to the sites of political parties and organisations, but these sites do offer ready access to what I referred to earlier as 'primary sources'.

The Internet is greater than the World Wide Web, and for many people *e-mail* is its greatest value. E-mail offers you ways of keeping in touch with your tutor and other students on your course. It is also the medium through which you might want to join one of the many *discussion groups* on political issues.

The high profile accorded to the computer-based learning resources means that they have tended to overshadow the more traditional electronic resources of *videos, television and radio*. These, however, can offer stimulation – via pictures and the spoken word – which the written word, which is still the main medium of the Internet, cannot do.

Recording and remembering learning

For all these learning resources, it is important to remember the points made earlier about active and deep learning. The latter is unlikely to occur if you just passively read the content of a book, article, CD-ROM database, or Internet web-site – or passively watch and listen to a television programme. You need to be interacting with your sources and this invariably means, in one way or another, making notes and finding ways of trying to remember what it is of value and importance from your learning.

Note-taking

The moment you sit down with a book, make sure you note down all the necessary bibliographical detail, including page numbers. Be sure to mark exact quotations in your notes. If you find something you may wish to quote word for word, make sure that you get every detail right, including the punctuation. If it contains what looks like an error, put [sic] after the error and then everyone will know that you are quoting accurately and the mistake is not yours. Much of your note-taking will consist of paraphrases or summaries of the text but often a passage from a book will spark off your own ideas. Make a note of the passage and write down your responses to the passage at once, or you will almost certainly forget what they were. Be sure that you make it very clear which notes are exact quotes, which are paraphrases and which are your own thoughts. (Use different colours of pen.) It is very easy, at a later date, to think an idea is your own when, in fact, you have picked it up in the course of your reading. Strangely, it is even possible to have an original idea and then to convince yourself that you read it somewhere.

Examples of Internet-based learning resources for Politics
(with a UK focus)

Search engines
All of the main search engines will provide a huge range of links on most issues relating to Politics. There is a dedicated classification of such sites at http://www.yahoo.com/ Social_Science/Political

'Jumping-off' points
There are a number of very useful gateway sites worth checking out for governmental and political organisations of all kinds, like the following:

Richard Kimber's Political Science Resources page at Keele University (UK) has an excellent reputation, http:// www.psr.keele.ac.uk

The Political Studies Association (UK), www.psa.ac.uk
The Internet Public Library, http://www.ipl.org
BritPolitics.com, http://www.britpolitics.com
Coverage of governments, parties and political organisations
worldwide, http://politicalresources.net
A good source of links from an American University (California
Stated Polytechnic University) can be found at http://
www.class.csupomona.edu/pls/research.htm

Official Government sites (UK examples)
Many UK official bodies are listed at http://www.open.gov.uk and
http://www.ukstate.com/
The Stationery Office web-site at *www.ukstate.com (The*
Stationery Office (TSO) was HMSO before its privatisation)
Office of the UK Prime Minister, http://www.number-10.gov.uk

Discussion groups on politics
There are numerous public newsgroups available on the
internet, which you can access through your newsreader (like
Outlook Express). These allow you to look in on discussions or
seek help and views. Here is a sample:

Alt.politics.british
Clari,web.world,gov.politics
Free.uk.politics.parties.conservative
Soc.parties.marxism
Uk.politics.constitution
Uk.politics.electoral
Uk.politics.philosophy
Us.politics

Notes are an aid to learning, not a substitute for it. You
should not just copy down words for future reference. Try to
take notes in your own words. Before you can do that, you have
to understand what you have read and that is the first step in
learning. The physical act of writing something down will help
to fix it in your mind. Also, you have to be selective and, in being
selective, you begin to exercise your critical judgement. If you
then take notes of your notes, you repeat these learning steps. If

you are using your own book or a photocopy, you will probably use highlighter pen, but don't be tempted to use highlighters as a substitute for making your own notes.

Tips for note taking

1. **Look for short cuts**. If you own the book or article (and only in such cases!), or if you can make a photocopy, use underlining or a highlighting pen to identify the content that you feel to be important or relevant to the task in hand (for example, material for an essay).

2. **Be selective.** Remember in this respect the distinctive aspects that I have argued as important in the study of Politics: concepts, theories, comparisons and competing ideas.

3. **Keep a full record of the source.** This is essential if you want to refer to it in coursework and should include the full details of the source and the page number from which a particular citation comes (and also how you can find it again, if necessary).

4. **Make clear when you are copying verbatim.** This will help to ensure that you do not plagiarise when you come to using your notes in coursework.

5. **Include your own thoughts.** These might be margin comments on connecting links to other sources, notes, topics, etc. or your thoughts on what you are reading – good or bad.

6. **File away systematically**. Use cardboard folders with dividers for notes made on loose pages, use an index box for notes made on cards, set up folders and sub-folders for word-processed notes.

7. **Be experimental.** Many of us feel safest with word-by-word copying of sentences but there are other ways of recording notes, especially ones that experiment with patterns and diagrams.

Remembering

Some people are fortunate in having excellent memories, but most of us struggle to remember what we are learning and get anxious about it. In the latter case, this is often because we have unrealistic expectations of what we need to remember. If our learning is organised and we keep reasonable records of what we have learnt, then there is no need to feel that this all needs to be recalled accurately from our brains. Instead, we should be confident about knowing where to find information when we need it. We also need to be aware that memory is not the same thing as intelligence or being knowledgeable. A good memory is of no great value if we lack the intellect to assess, analyse and use information in appropriate ways. And the more knowledge we gain of a particular subject, the more we realise how little we really know and how much more there is that still needs to be discovered and understood.

Improving your concentration

For one week keep a time record of your learning. After each learning session – in class, in the library, at home and so on – reflect on how well you concentrated and what things distracted your attention. Look for any patterns in these results – do they relate to the time of day, the length of time of your study period, the amount of variety in your learning, or the impact of your surroundings? Consider how these patterns suggest ways of improving your concentration.

Memory only becomes of vital importance in examinations and tests and I shall offer some advice later on this. For most other things, your memory will look after itself, especially if you adopt the strategic learning approaches recommended earlier. There is, however, one other important point and that relates to your attention span. Learning, and remembering what you have learnt, does depend on your attentiveness (in the lecture or to reading a book, for example). Being attentive in learning means concentrating. Again, it is not so much an issue that some people are better than others at concentrating. We are all capable of concentrating on our studies but how well will depend on how interested we are, how stimulating the learning material is, and whether we are in 'the right frame of mind'.

Self-directed learning

Libraries are usually good places to work, if you can manage to ignore occasional irritating whisperers. They should put you in the mood for learning and are free of the distractions there might be when reading at home. If you are used to working in the library, you get into the habit of using it in breaks between classes, potentially useful time which can easily be frittered away.

When learning at home (maybe in a flat with other students), make sure that there are clear rules about not interrupting your study time. Ask those living with you to be considerate about your exams and essay deadlines and make sure you do the same for them if they are also studying.

By now you will be aware of the length of time that you can work without a break. You are unlikely to be working effectively if you go for much more than an hour without a rest. You can keep your concentration up for longer if you vary your tasks. Read and takes notes for a bit. Then do some practical exercises or test yourself in some other way before going back to reading again. Remember not to set yourself too much reading in one go.

Sit down to study with a realistic target in mind. Reward yourself (with a rest, a shower, a computer game, a chat with friends or a phone call) when you have achieved your goal.

Try to avoid working late at night. If you find that it is becoming a habit, revise your time management. If you do find yourself burning the midnight oil, and all students do from time to time, strong black coffee or other highly caffeinated drinks are not the answer. They may give you a short boost, but they will leave you even more tired and so you have another cup, and another. The result is that when you finally go to bed you can't sleep and you will probably get a headache as well. Try herbal tea or a few deep breaths at an open window instead.

ASSESSMENT STRATEGIES

Although I have separated out assessment from learning, it is important to recognise that they are vitally interconnected. You may be dreading the thought of having to write essays, take examinations and other forms of assessment, but there are good reasons why they are such an important part of your university education. First and foremost they provide you with an opportunity to get feedback on your learning from your tutors about how well you understand a topic and are able to organise your knowledge about it. Second, they require you to engage with what you have learnt by having to communicate it to others. Assessments also require you to assimilate your learning by drawing knowledge and ideas from a variety of sources and putting them together from a particular angle. And finally, the skills you will be developing in your assessment are highly transferable to other settings, be they work or personal (see Chapter 8).

At one time, assessments in universities were wholly based on unseen examinations, usually of three hours. And degree 'finals', as they were called, could consist of anything up to a dozen three-hour papers taken over a period of about two weeks. Today you are likely to experience a wide variety of assessments spread over the years of your course, and you may even avoid the traditional examinations.

Like learning, there is a tool kit of strategies that will help if you learn to use them. (You wouldn't dream of trying to repair a car without the right tools and some understanding of how to use them; the same should be the case for undertaking university assessments.) The tool kits for some of the kinds of assessments you will be experiencing in the study of Politics are outlined below and you should consider following some of these up in greater detail in the general study skills books and guides available in your library.

Examinations

Being successful in examinations, like most things in life, is best achieved by knowing about, and practising, the special skills involved. It is not just about having a good memory. It is much more about following the kind of guidance offered below.

Each kind of examination will require variations in terms of the tool kit of skills for being successful but all can be broken down to the following common stages: long-term preparation; short-term revision; and the examination itself. The following table attempts to summarise what you should be aiming to do at each stage.

Examination tool kit

Stages of the examination process	Tool kit
Long-term preparation (starting from the beginning of the course or module)	1. Collate your personal learning materials, including lecture handouts, lecture notes, seminar papers and notes, annotated photocopies, newspaper cuttings, essays and so on. 2. Copy the syllabus to which the examination relates. 3. Collect examples of questions from previous examinations and try giving yourself five minutes to do an outline plan for an answer. 4. Organise your learning materials around the main topics in the syllabus – with indications showing links and cross references 5. Periodically, skim through your learning materials to keep them fresh in your mind.

Short-term revision (at least two weeks prior to the examination)	1. Summarise your notes on the topics that are likely to come up in the examination (trying to distil your notes down – in stages if necessary – to no more than one side of A4 paper per topic, preferably in diagrammatic form). You can also have a final look at these before going into the exam.
	2. Commit to memory your distilled diagram for each topic which should contain key concepts (and the buzz words that need to go into their definition), names of major authors you want to show you have read, strengths and weaknesses of competing perspectives. Try to use the first letter of each point to make up a mnemonic.
	3. Do past papers. You might like to brainstorm a few past papers with friends to get ideas on how to structure answers, and at some point, when you are far enough on with your revision, but well before the examination date, set yourself a paper under exam conditions.
	4. Prioritise your time at this stage on topics that you feel less interested or confident in but which you know you can't avoid. Finish your preparations for these first, otherwise you may put them off until it is too late.
	5. Make sure that you have revised enough topics and that these include at least one more than the number of questions you will have to answer in case one of your chosen topics does not come up or the question is asked in a way you don't like.
	6. Make sure you know where and when the exam is. If you are not a morning person, get an alarm call or ask someone to see that you are up in time.
In the examination	1. Get there in plenty of time so that you arrive feeling calm and confident, but do not get there too early; you do not want to hang about with a crowd of hysterical people working themselves into a nervous frenzy. Be sure you have everything you need: identification if required, watch, spare pens, and handkerchief!

2. Check the instructions for the examination to check how many questions you need to attempt and whether the examination paper is divided into parts.

3. If there is anything you need to ask the invigilator, just put your hand up. It does occasionally happen that misprints occur on exam papers, in spite of careful proof-reading. If something is missed out from the instructions, or they are not clear, the invigilator will be glad to hear about it and will inform the rest of the class. If you run out of paper, feel unwell, need to go to the toilet, or need to borrow a pen, put your hand up and the invigilator will come to you.

4. Read through all the questions thoroughly (don't just look for a buzz word and start writing all you know about it).

5. Decide on questions to be answered, and what order you are going to do them in.

6. Check the amount of time to be given to each question (remember that the early part of your answer is likely to gain the bulk of your grade and after a certain point you are not really improving your grade and that this time would be better spent on the early stages of another question).

7. Don't go overboard on your first and favourite question at the expense of other questions you are required to do.

8. Make sure you attempt all the questions required (if you make no attempt on a question you can only get zero for it and therefore will not be marked out of total of 100%). If you really are running out of time, get as much down as possible for your final question in note form, under the headings Introduction, Development and Conclusion.

9. Think before you start to write and draft out a short plan, including key terms.

10. Structure your answers as you would do for an essay.

11. Keep checking the wording of the question to make sure your answers remain relevant (try periodically bringing the words of the question back into the answer).

12. Remember that your examiners want you to pass. They are actively looking forward to rewarding you for displaying relevant knowledge. It looks bad on them if their students don't do well!
13. Do a final check at the end of the exam to make sure that you have put your name and other details required on your answer book.

If you follow this advice, you will cope well with your examinations, and maybe surprise yourself with the grades you get. If nothing else, remember that poor marks in exams are primarily due to one or more of the following:

1. Not reading the instructions and doing one question too few or one too many.
2. Not reading the question.
3. Bad time management.
4. Irrelevant content, that is NOT answering the question.
5. Trying to substitute made-up waffle for fact.
6. Not giving enough examples.

Make sure that these do not apply to you!

Essays and dissertations

You did not get as far as considering university entrance without having gained some skill in writing, but learning to write well is a lifelong task. During your time at university, you will be expected to polish your formal writing style and adapt to the particular conventions of the subject you are writing about.

At university, you will be assessed primarily on what you write and that is inseparable from how you write, because it does not matter how much you know if you cannot get that knowledge down on paper in a way that makes sense to the reader.

Make the most of available technology. Many university departments insist on the use of word processors for essays and you should take advantage of computing courses for new students.

Why write essays?
The obvious answer is 'to prove that you have learnt something'. That, however, is not the only or the best answer. If you tackle your essays in the right way, you will find that they are, in fact, a very important part of the learning process. It is only when you try to explain things in a totally clear and unambiguous way that you begin to expose the gaps in your understanding. More encouragingly, you may find that, as you arrange your ideas, you make connections that you had not seen before. You are putting what you have learnt to work and gaining confidence in handling your new knowledge. The more effort you put into an essay, the more you will benefit.

Essay-writing at university level demands knowledge of the conventions of academic discourse and especially of the way of writing accepted within the academic circle of your particular subject. All academic discourse demands attention to detail, not just in the facts and theories you present, but also in the manner of presentation. A consistent level of formality is required and an impersonal style where the writer does not get in the way of the subject is strongly recommended. Vocabulary and grammar have to be carefully checked to make sure there is no possibility of misunderstandings (see the next chapter). Bibliographies and sources have to be cited. In short, you need to become expert in the transferable skills of gathering, selecting, organising and communicating information.

First read the question
More good students get bad marks because they misread the question than for any other reason. There are certain recognisable types: Discuss . . . , Compare and contrast . . . , Describe . . . Analyse . . . . Think about it. Make sure you undertake the activity asked for.

Everything you write must be relevant to the question. If you include irrelevancies, they will not gain marks and they will even lose marks by taking up space that should have been used on answering the question. Word limits on essays are based on the assumption that every word is necessary and to the point. Lecturers think very, very hard about the exact wording of questions. If you are in any doubt what an essay question means, do not be afraid to ask whoever set it.

Choose your question wisely. With experience, you will discover the kind of question you are best at.

The writing process
Writing is not a single big task. It is a lot of little tasks:

1. Collecting data
2. Finding a structure
3. Making a draft
4. Polishing
5. Preparing for submission
6. Proof-reading

Sources
Most of the information you need will have been covered in lectures and reinforced in seminars and tutorials. A good essay, however, shows signs of additional reading which has obviously been well understood and used appropriately.

Taking notes for essays
When taking notes, keep the exact wording of the essay title in front of you. Constantly ask yourself, 'How does what I'm reading relate to the title?' Noting down your initial reactions to what you are reading can be a good way of getting into the actual writing of your essay.

Since academic writing demands that you provide proper bibliographies listing all the works you have consulted, it is particularly important that you record all the necessary bibliographic details. If you take something off the internet, make sure you record the website and the date you accessed it.

Finding a structure
Students are usually surprised at how much importance markers attach to the structure of essays. Anybody can regurgitate facts. That is not what essay-writing is about.

Markers are looking for the ability to put the facts to work. Different subjects place a slightly different emphasis on the way facts are manipulated but, in general, you are expected to construct some kind of argument. In this context, argument does not necessarily mean anything confrontational. It simply means that your essay should have a thread running through it.

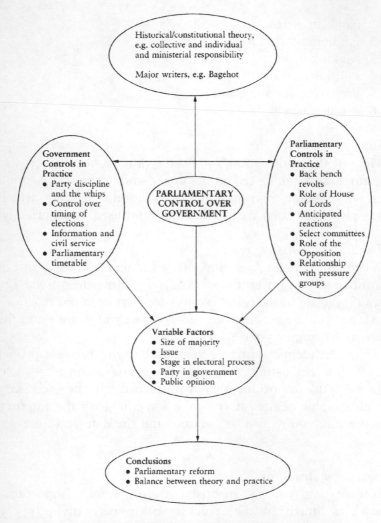

Example of a mind map for preparing an essay

Sometimes the wording of an essay title suggests a structure. Assume you have been given the essay title *Critically evaluate the view that the UK Parliament no longer has any effective control over the British Government.* This suggests the need for a brief introduction, a major section expounding the view, a critique section and a conclusion. If no obvious structure suggests itself, experiment with different ways of writing an essay plan.

Some people use mind maps. Put the core idea down on the middle of a bit of paper and let other ideas branch off, as in the example for the question on parliamentary control over the government. These secondary ideas might generate their own branches. Little clusters start to form. These might each form a section or paragraph of your argument. Do not worry if the same idea crops up in two places but ask yourself if that produces a possible link between sections.

You might prefer a more linear plan, like a flow chart, or you might try grouping related facts, listing pros and cons, identifying major themes, and so on. These strategies may uncover such possible orders as: a logical progression as a proof unfolds; a chronological progression moving linearly backwards or forwards in time; a spatial structure, dealing with different geographic or topographic areas; a movement from the general to the particular, perhaps stating a hypothesis and testing it on specific examples; or moving from the particular to the general, constructing a hypothesis from the evidence you have set out.

If no plan emerges, do not despair. Sometimes the act of writing brings the necessary insights. Get started on free writing. To do this, just write as fast as you can, without stopping to think, without lifting your pen, for at least three minutes. It doesn't matter if you write nonsense. At least you have something on paper to expand, re-order and improve.

If you still cannot see a way of making all the data hang together as a whole instead of a jumble of facts, seek help from your tutor.

First draft
The first sentence is always the hardest. A good way to tackle the opening paragraph is to put the question into your own

words or say what you understand by it and prepare your reader for the way you are going to answer it. It will help your reader to understand your essay if you give an overview of where you are heading. You could state your objectives or list the main issues you intend to deal with (in the order that they appear in your essay) or say briefly what you intend to explain or discuss. In this opening paragraph you want to get the reader on your side by arousing interest.

If you are having difficulty getting started, remember that you do not have to start at the beginning. Some of the ideas that you have jotted down whilst reading and note-taking can be written out to form a series of nuclei around which you can build up your text. Then you can fit them into your planned structure

If the words still will not come, try talking. Explain what you are trying to write, to your flatmate, or even recording your thoughts onto a cassette. Write it down exactly as you said it.

Ideas are like buses – either none come or they all come at once. So, when you have plenty of ideas, just concentrate on getting them all down. Whether you use a word processor or pen and paper, just enjoy the experience. Worry about spelling, grammar, the exact words later. An essay which overflows with ideas and has to be refined is better than one that has to be padded out.

Stay flexible. What you write may give you new inspiration. You may find connections you had not noticed before and you may need to revise your essay plan a bit. It is very easy to move chunks of text around on your word processor; experimenting with structure is not a problem. Read it over to check that the section you have moved links into its new surroundings.

The final paragraph should not introduce any new material or any new ideas. An old recipe for an essay structure is:

1. Say what you are going to say
2. Say it
3. Say what you have said

This plan has been sneered at as over-simplified but there is a lot of sense in it. In particular, you will not go far wrong if your closing paragraph briefly restates the question and says how you have answered it. If you cannot show in your final paragraph that you have answered the question, perhaps you should ask yourself if you really have done so.

Make absolutely sure that everything you say is relevant. If necessary, point out why it is relevant. By now the essay title ought to be engraved on your heart. But just check again to make sure you have not lost sight of it. Is your essay a discussion, a comparison, or evidence in support of a hypothesis? Is that what was asked for?

Polishing
Effective communication is what makes good writers stand out. When you are writing essays, it is very easy to fall into the trap of thinking that this is between you and the page and you forget that a real person is going to have to read it and perhaps even enjoy it. Consider your reader.

Your reader is a well-informed academic who is going to take you and your essay seriously. The style is therefore formal. This does not mean that it has to be long-winded. It is very often the people who understand their subject best who can explain it most simply and directly. Those who have only half a grasp of what they are talking about are the ones who are most likely to dress up their shallow knowledge in dense language. They think they know what they want to say, but when it comes to putting it down on paper, the words won't come because they have not thought everything through. If you can say what you mean with absolute clarity, you will demonstrate your knowledge effectively. Look at every single sentence you write and ask yourself whether it is crystal clear. Trying to achieve this clarity will often expose a lack of understanding on your part and that is what makes essay-writing such a good learning opportunity. You expose the gaps and work on them. Do not be tempted to fudge.

Murphy's Law of Writing: if your readers can misunderstand something they will. (And Murphy was an optimist.)

Preparing for submission
A departmental style sheet telling you how to set your work out is
often given in a class booklet. If not, here are a few suggestions:

1. Make sure your typeface is big enough:

> You could use 8 pt for footnotes at a pinch
> but 10 pt is just about the limit that older eyes can read
> comfortably for any length of time.
> 12 pt is easy on the eye (especially for ageing
> academics who have a lot of essays to read).

2. A page with plenty of white space is more attractive than a
black, solid block of text. Make sure you use big margins so
that the marker can write helpful comments. Separate your
paragraphs with a blank line instead of indenting.

3. If you are quoting more than three lines of prose, you should
indent the quotation:

> It is not enough to attain a degree of precision which a
> person reading in good faith can understand, but it is
> necessary to attain if possible to a degree of precision
> which a person reading in bad faith cannot misunder-
> stand. (Stephen 1890)

This may be combined with a change of size:

> Moreover, you need to choose the right words in order that
> you may make your meaning clear not only to your reader but
> also to yourself. The first requisite for any writer is to know
> just what meaning he wants to convey, and it is only by
> clothing his thoughts in words that he can think at all. (Gowers
> 1987)

Note that, when indentation is used for a quotation, there are
no quotation marks.

4. Imaginative use of fonts may help to make a point but, for the main body of your text, avoid weird and wonderful fonts.

Footnotes or endnotes

Your departmental style sheet may give a ruling on this. If not, try to do whatever helps the reader. It is an irritation constantly having to flick to the end of a text. On the other hand, too many footnotes on a page can make for a very ugly appearance. For a few short notes which are important to the understanding of the text, the foot of the page is best. If they are copious and more for form than necessity, tuck them away at the end.

References and bibliographies

The purpose of references and bibliographies is to enable your readers to find for themselves the material to which you have referred. They may want to check your accuracy or, more positively, they may be stimulated by your writing to go and find out more. Whenever you are picking up another's idea, even if you are not using exact words, it is usual to use the author's surname, the date of publication and the page number in brackets (Author 1999: 999) after the citation or, if the author's name is part of your text, just bracket the date and the page number: as in this example by Author (1999: 999). If an author has more than one publication of the same date, these are designated 1999a and 1999b and so on. Proper referencing is essential if you are not to be accused of plagiarism.

Plagiarism, whether intentional or unintentional, is a form of cheating which universities are very concerned about and they are increasingly vigilant to ensure that students do not copy work from other students, from published sources or from the internet. There are even computer programs designed to detect plagiarism. Of course you will present and discuss other people's ideas, opinions and theories in your essay, but you must say where you found them and you must be very careful not to claim them as your own original thoughts.

Bibliographies are a horrible chore but the task can be made a lot easier if you note all the necessary information right from the very beginning of your research. It is soul-destroying chasing round libraries looking for things like page numbers and place of publication when the rest of the job is done.

The perfectionist will ensure that the latest editions of books are consulted wherever possible but, if you cannot get hold of the most recent edition, list in your bibliography the one that you actually referred to.

If you are referring to a web-site, you must make sure that you give enough information to make sure that a reader could access the same site. Give the date in case the site has been updated since you used it.

The exact formats for bibliographies vary greatly and attention should be paid to where stops, commas and other punctuation marks are used. Your university department should give advice on the referencing style you will be expected to use. A widely accepted style is known as the Harvard system and some examples of this follow.

Harvard system of reference (some examples)

Author, A. N. (1996) *Book Title in Italics. Place: Publisher.*

Author, A. N. (1996a) 'Article title without capitals'. *Italicised Journal Name*, 10 (3), pp. 1–55.

Author, A. N. (1996b) **In** 'An essay in a book' S. Cribble (ed.) *Book Title.* Place: Publisher, pp. 1–55.

Author, A. N. (1996c) 'An Internet source' [online] URL: http://www.xxxxx.xxx. [Date accessed].

Proof-reading
Always proof-read on a hard copy. You will need to proof-read several times because you cannot do all the tasks at once.

Stage one: Take a break. It is very difficult to proof-read your own work and the more of a distance you can put between writing and re-reading the better.

Stage two: Read for general sense and good communication. Read it out loud. Are there any bits that are unclear, get your tongue in a twist or sound rather pompous? At this stage, do not stop to correct things or you will lose the big picture. Just make a mark in the margin. Have you got the balance right, spending most time on the most important points? Once you have read right through, wrestle with the awkward sentences. Be careful that any improvements you make do not introduce new errors. When you are sure you have done everything for your reader that you would like an author to do for you, you may proceed to the next stage.

Stage three: Do the mechanical bits in turn. Use the spellchecker but do your own check for things that it will miss like *it's/its*, *where/were*. A very common kind of mistake is to mistype the little words, *on* instead of *of* for example. Is your punctuation helpful? Work out all the sums, double check names and dates, physically look up everything that you have cross-referenced. When checking your grammar, common errors to look out for include verbs changing tense and pronouns drifting between *one* and *you*, sentences without verbs, run-on sentences where there should be a full stop in the middle, singular verbs with plural subjects and singular subjects with plural verbs.

Stage four: Give it to someone else to read, not necessarily a specialist in your subject. Ask them to make sure they can completely understand every sentence. In this way, they will test your own understanding. (Offer to do the same for them. You can learn a lot about your own writing from helping to make other people's writing clearer.)

Have a well-earned rest and look forward to an excellent mark. Then, when you get your essay back, resist the temptation to put it away in a file. Look at the comments carefully. If a few of you can get together and read each others' essays after marking you get a much better understanding of what makes a good essay in your subject.

Complete disaster

What do you do if, in spite of all the good advice in this book, you fail to hand your essay in on time? You may have a good reason, such as illness. If so, you should provide a medical certificate. Your director of studies or personal tutor should be notified of serious personal problems that interfere with your work and they may be taken into account if you find you need an extension. Having three essays to hand in for the same day does not constitute grounds for an extension. It is merely a fact of university life and a very good reason for organising your time wisely. As soon as you feel you are behind schedule, have a word with your tutor.

If the worst comes to the worst, face up to it. Go to your tutor, lecturer or course organiser, own up and apologise. The longer you leave it, the harder it will be. Do *not* try to explain how your hard disk ate your essay at the last moment; you should have kept a floppy copy. Nobody believes that computers crash two hours before the submission time. By that late hour you should have a copy already printed out for a final proof-read. You could hand that copy in if the computer crashes. Better to hand in a late draft than a draft late. You may find that you will be marked down for late submission but, if you have ignored all this advice, that is exactly what you deserve!

Other kinds of writing

Essays are the most demanding pieces of writing that you will be asked to do in first year. In later years, you may be asked to do a much longer dissertation and you may even want to write papers for conferences or articles for publication. Essay-writing trains you for these activities. The processes are just the same. If you keep the needs of your reader in mind, you will be able to write for all occasions.

1. Make yourself comfortable in a distraction-free zone.
2. Use mind maps, flow charts, etc. to help you make plans.
3. Start writing as soon as you start researching.
4. Try free writing or talking to get started or to unblock you if you get stuck.
5. Ask for help if you need it.

Finally, have a look at the following mock feedback to two fictitious students. Are you going to be a Geri Mander or a Polly Tickle?

Oral presentations

Increasingly, students in higher education are assessed through presentations. There is a long tradition of students being required to deliver papers in seminars as the basis for group discussion. It is only in more recent years that students have been assessed both on the content of these papers and how well they have been delivered. Assessing the delivery of presentations has been introduced in recognition that the role of universities includes equipping students with skills that can later be transferred to other aspects of their lives (more on this in the next chapter). There is no doubt that for most students this is a stressful part of their studies, but it shouldn't come as a surprise that many later report back to their tutors how helpful their 'training' in presentations had been at job interviews or for speaking at a public meeting.

Being successful in presentations depends primarily on good preparation, not only of the content but also in how it is going to be delivered. For the latter, there is no good alternative to practising by giving your presentation to some friends or even to yourself in front of a mirror with the stopwatch running. Learn by observation of your tutors and other students some of the tricks of the trade. There is an example of the criteria that might be used to grade your presentation on page 173.

University of Coketown, Department of Politics
Coursework Assessment Feedback

Critically examine the view that the UK Parliament no longer has any effective control over the British Government.

Assessment Criteria	Feedback Comments	Feedback Comments
	GERI MANDER	POLLY TICKLE
1. Specific criteria Contains examples drawn from current Politics in the UK	You have mentioned the examples given in the lecture but have not added any of your own.	I liked the inclusion of references to the recent feature articles in *The Guardian*, but you could have questioned their objectivity.
Goes beyond textbook content	Your essay is little more than a regurgitation of the lecture and shows very little evidence of wider reading, other than the set textbook.	The material you included from the recent article in *Political Studies* was very helpful.
Recognises problematic nature of the terms Parliament and Government	You do attempt to define the two terms in your introduction but do not then go on to see how different aspects of the two lead to different conclusions, e.g. between the role of the Commons and the Lords.	You recognised the need to separate out discussion on the Lords and the Commons, and rightly emphasised the latter. I didn't feel, however, that you really got to grips with the term Government and much of your essay was concerned with only the Prime Minister and the Cabinet.
2. Structure, organisation, and presentation of coursework	Your introduction is OK in that it includes a definition of the terms in the question but it does not set out how you have structured your approach to the question. This is perhaps because there is no clear organisation to your essay, which really is little more than a list of more or less relevant points. The fact that you did not attempt a conclusion summing up the arguments relating to the question compounded the weakness in your essay structuring.	Your assignment was well structured with clear signposts to show the reader how you are moving from one point to another. It was clear from your introduction how you organised your content. The main section of your essay was organised well using the 'for and against' approach and the way you dealt with these thematically was very good – particularly the theme relating to party discipline. Your conclusion, however, was a bit thin and could have summarised better the contrasting perspectives on the question.
3. Use of sources (including referencing and bibliography)	You have provided quite a lengthy bibliography but there is no evidence in your essay that you have read most of the sources.	Good range of sources used and well referenced. You must remember, though, to give page numbers when you are referencing actual quotations.
4. Application of theory, use of principles and concepts	Your list of points is largely factual and you don't relate them clearly to the central concept of accountability or to theories about the relationship between the executive and the legislative.	You brought out very well the central importance of the concept of 'accountability' and defined it well. I did feel, though, that you could have tied this in more fully to the theory of democracy.
5. Evidence of analytical, critical and independent thinking	For all the above reasons, your essay was largely descriptive and did not show any attempt to look for connections between points covered. At the end, it is not clear whether you agree or disagree with the view in the question.	The way you broke the question down demonstrated your analytic ability and your conclusion rightly concluded that the view in the question is highly questionable. I think you lost an opportunity in your conclusion to offer some independent insight.
6. Personal and practical skills	There are a lot of careless mistakes in your essay which suggests you did not proof-read it (did you use a spell check?). You need to break down your over-lengthy paragraphs by separating them into one paragraph for each major point.	Very well word-processed assignment with excellent spelling and punctuation. Pay attention, though, to your use of overlong sentences which sometimes get you into difficulties with your grammar.
Grade	F	B+

University of Coketown, Department of Politics
Assessment Criteria for presentations

Module		Student	
	Criteria		Feedback
Was the presentation delivered in a lively style (not just reading an essay)?			
Did the student make eye contact with the audience?			
Was there good use of relevant visual aids?			
Did the student keep to the allocated time limit?			
Did the student keep the attention of the audience?			
Was the language appropriate, e.g. avoiding jargon?			
Was the evidence presented clearly?			
Did the student respond well to questions?			
Grade:			

Other forms of assessment

You may well come across other forms of assessment on your Politics course: you will almost certainly have to write a *dissertation* if you are majoring in the subject, you may have to write *reports* on those politics programmes which give a strong emphasis to public administration, and may also get involved in *problem-solving* exercises. These, like those discussed above, imply that they are individual assessments, but you may well also find yourself involved in *group work*-based assessments. Groups are at the heart of the political process and it is something of a law in Politics that influence grows exponentially when people act collectively: the larger the group the greater their influence usually is. It is therefore fitting that Politics students should be given some opportunity to develop their skills in working in groups. Why not, therefore, approach you group work assessments as a practising political scientist? Take on the part of a 'participant observer' – as well as a group actor – and consider the following:

1. What were the sources of conflict in the group?
2. What processes were used to resolve this conflict?
3. Were the concepts of power, authority and influence in evidence?
4. What roles did people take (leader, facilitator, resistor, avoider)?
5. Were decisions arrived at democratically or autocratically?
6. How effective was the group in meeting its objectives?
7. Were there any unanticipated outcomes of the group activity?
8. Was my contribution to the group positive, negative or neutral?

More on this in the next chapter.

Computing, information technology and assessment

In addition to their value as a learning resource, computers can also make a major contribution to the efficiency and effectiveness of preparing your assessment, that is making them easier and better. The most obvious application is in *word-processing*. Not only are word-processed assignments clearer to read, the drafting of them is made so much easier by the ability to edit your work (without the need for a total rewriting or retyping) and to check your work for both spelling and grammatical errors. By using the computer to store your assessments, notes and downloaded documents, you can use the files created to search out links (using the Find facility) and to cut and paste from one source to another (remembering of course to reference when this is not in your own words). If you are not proficient in word-processing you should seek out opportunities provided by your college to undertake training. This training will help by advising you on the layout of documents (the key point here is to keep it simple and avoid too many embellishments). The training will also help in opening up more complex aspects of word-processing. An example would be the ability to set out an essay in outline view first, identifying the various sections of your essay (introduction, development and conclusion) and the sub-headings for the main points to be included in each section. This helps to give a structure to your essay from an early stage. You can always delete the headings later if they are not needed.

For your essays, and especially for your presentations, the inclusion of some graphical content can add significantly to the quality of your work. This might take the form of tables and graphs prepared in a *spreadsheet* application and pasted into your document, or diagrams that you have prepared using the draw facility present in most word-processing programmes. For presentation purposes all of these could be pasted into a presentation package like Microsoft PowerPoint, and if your classroom is fully equipped you can use the computer to present your material.

I suggested an exercise earlier on managing your time that could very effectively be done on a personal information manager. For more complex planning of your work you could try out a project management package. For keeping a track of your references you could try using a referencing programme like Endnote.

Given the rapid developments in the capacity and availability of computing, its value as a tool for both learning and assessment is still at the early stage of development. By the time you complete your course you may well find that its applications goes far beyond those presented here.

SUMMARY

Congratulations if you have got to the end of this chapter. If you have read it all, then well done. But if you have just used it to dip into the parts relevant to you, that's fine also. Hopefully some of the content will continue to be relevant after your introductory year as a Politics student. Learning to learn, and developing the associated skills, is not a one-off task. It is something we continue to develop throughout our lives, and hopefully not just when we are taking a formal course of study.

The key message of this chapter, and of the approach to study that is recommended, is that the successful student of Politics is:

P repared
O rganised
L earned
I nformed
T houghtful
I nterested
C onfident
S trategic

The next chapter tries to demonstrate that these qualities are of equal relevance to the world of work, and to life generally. You may be *getting set* to study Politics, but it does no harm to consider from the outset what this might be leading to after you have graduated. So please read on.

FURTHER READING

There are a large number of study skills publications available for students entering higher education. As it has been not possible to give full coverage to all the learning and assessment strategies in this chapter, I would encourage you to follow up your reading by referring to one or more of the books below.

Atkinson, Brian, Barry McCarthy and Ken Phillips (1987) *Studying Society. An Introduction to Social Science*. Oxford: Oxford University Press.

Barrass, Robert (1984) *A Guide to Effective Study, Revision and Examination Techniques*. London: Chapman Hall.

Bourner, Tom and Phil Race (1995) *How to Win as a Part-time Student: A Study Skills Guide*. London: Kogan Page.

Crème, Phyllis and Mary Lea (1997) *Writing at University: A guide for students*. Buckingham: Open University Press.

Dunleavy, Patrick (1986) *Studying for a Degree in the Humanities and Social Sciences*. London: Macmillan.

Freeman, Richard (1991) *Mastering Study Skills*. London: Macmillan.

Gowers, Sir Ernest (1987) *The Complete Plain Words*. Harmondsworth: Penguin.

Honey, P. and Alan Mumford (1992) *Manual of Learning Styles*. Maidenhead: P. Honey.

Kolb, David A. (1984) *Experimental Learning*. Englewood Cliffs, NJ: Prentice-Hall.

Laqueur, Walter (1971) *Dictionary of Politics*. London: Weidenfeld and Nicolson.

Lashley, Conrad (1995) *Improving Study Skills. A Competence Approach*. London: Cassell.

Marshall, Lorraine and Frances Rowland (1993) *A Guide to Learning Independently* (second edition). Buckingham: Open University Press.

Morgan, Alastair (1995) *Improving Your Students' Learning: Reflections on the Experience of Study*. London: Kogan Page.

Northedge, Andrew (1992) *The Good Study Guide*. Milton Keynes: Open University.

Pask, Gordon (1978) 'Styles and strategies of learning'. *British Journal of Educational Psychology*. 1976, no. 46, pp. 128–48.

Renwick, Alan and Ian Swinburn (1987) *Basic Political Concepts* (second edition). London: Stanley Thornes (Publishers) Ltd.

Roberts, Geoffrey (1971) *Dictionary of Political Analysis*. Harlow: Longman.

Robertson, David (1993) *Penguin Dictionary of Politics*. Harmondsworth: Penguin.

Rowntree, Derek (1998) *Learn How To Study*. London: Warner Books.

Winship, Ian and Alison McNab (1998) *The Student's Guide to the Internet 1998*. London: Library Association Publishing.

The University of Northumberland at Newcastle maintains an excellent and very comprehensive web-site with links on study skills: http://online.northumbria.ac.uk/central_departments/student_services/study_skills/studskil.htm

The British Library of Political and Economic Science maintains an interesting web-site entitled *Internet Politician* and provides guidance on Internet skills for politicians: http://www.sosig.ac.uk/vts/politician/start.htm

8 KEY SKILLS AND EMPLOYABILITY

OK, so you've done very well and got a good degree in Politics! But what use are you going to be to me and my organisation?

If you have recently taken A and AS levels as part of the new Curriculum 2000 post-GCSE arrangements then you will already know about key skills, and maybe had to prepare a portfolio of your achievements. If you have followed a more vocational route after GCSEs then key skills will have formed an important part of your studies. If you are a mature student then the terminology that follows may be new to you.

There is a strong chance that the majority of you will be sceptical about the importance of key skills, and maybe hoping to escape from them in higher education. No chance! And for very good reasons. The earlier chapters of this book have introduced you to the main fields of enquiry within the discipline of Politics. But the chances are that you will not be able to remember most of your learning after you graduate and are unlikely to be working in a field where the specific knowledge you have gained is required. You will also find, especially in the field of Politics, that the political world you studied is constantly changing and that some of your knowledge will rapidly become dated. None of this means that your studies have been wasted. In addition to your knowledge and understanding of Politics and how to update it, you will also have gained a range of very important skills that are immediately transferable to the both the world of work and to your life generally.

The purpose of this chapter is to help you to recognise the skills and abilities that you will gain from studying Politics at university, and to be able to speak about them in response to

178

the kind of question that was posed at the beginning of the chapter. I want to help make explicit the full extent of the skills you will gain as a student of Politics. I will also identify the range and choice of career opportunities after your Politics degree. The chapter concludes with a brief discussion on how you might use your knowledge and skills in the actual practice of politics.

Please read on, and remember:

Key skills are important

1. They will be gained as part of your university study of Politics.

2. They are transferable to the world of work and to life generally.

3. They may well be of more lasting value than the knowledge and understanding gained about the subject of Politics.

4. Employers will expect you to be clear about the skills gained as part of your degree studies.

5. Improving them will help to boost your confidence.

Using the knowledge that you have already gained about different political perspectives, could you argue the case for key skills in higher education from the standpoint of the New Right (think about the needs of the economy), New Labour (think also about their value in terms of widening participation to socially and economically disadvantaged groups) and Liberal Democrats (think about individual freedom and fulfilment)? Is your conclusion, that there is a consensus (agreement) on their desirability but for different reasons?

If you are still not convinced, the following statements on expected outcomes from Politics and International Relations degrees have been published as a national benchmark for all universities by the national Quality Assurance Agency:

Generic intellectual skills

Graduates in Politics and International Relations will be able to:

- gather, organize and deploy evidence, data and information from a variety of secondary and some primary sources;

- identify, investigate, analyse, formulate and advocate solutions to problems;

- construct reasoned argument, synthesize relevant information and exercise critical judgement;

- reflect on their own learning and seek and make use of constructive feedback;

- manage their own learning self-critically.

Personal transferable skills

Graduates in Politics and International Relations will be able to:

- communicate effectively and fluently in speech and writing;

- use communication and information technology for the retrieval and presentation of information, including, where appropriate, statistical or numerical information;

- work independently, demonstrating initiative, self-organization and time-management;

- collaborate with others to achieve common goals.

Extract from benchmark statements for Politics and International Relations (QAA, 2002)

THE SIX TRANSFERABLE SKILLS

There is general agreement that there are six key skills which need to be developed as part of the wider activity of learning. The first three are regarded as 'core' and most commonly taught and assessed in schools and colleges while the final three are referred to as 'wider skills' and are less formally taught and assessed.

The six key skills

1. Communication

2. Application of number

3. Information technology

4. Working with others

5. Improving own learning and performance

6. Problem-solving

For the major part of this chapter you will be given guidance on the meaning of these skills and provided with examples of how to develop them as part of your study of Politics.

What I want to emphasise is that these skills are not something you will be practising and developing in addition to your study of Politics; you will be doing this *as part of* your studies, often without fully realising you are doing so. All the evidence of research into key skills and higher education points to one clear conclusion: that students develop these skills best when they are part of (that is, embedded within) the curriculum.

You should already have spotted a clear link between these skills and the previous chapter on study skills. This is a good example of how skills are embedded in your learning in higher education, and how you can make explicit to other people the skills that you have gained.

The following table illustrates the relationship between key skills, the previous chapter on study skills and the content of the following sections.

Links between study and key skills

The six key skills	Study skills (previous chapter)	Key skills (this chapter)
Written and oral communication	Writing essays and dissertations Oral presentations	Improving communication: a basic primer
Application of Number		Understanding tables of figures and doing calculations
Information technology	Learning from computing and information technology Computing and information technology and assessment	IT skills checklist
Working with others		Issues about group work
Improving own learning and performance	Learning strategically Learning independently Learning from lectures Learning from seminars and tutorials Learning from the printed word Recording and remembering learning Self-directed learning Assessment strategies	Time management
Problem-solving		Thinking rationally

WRITTEN AND ORAL COMMUNICATION: A SHORT PRIMER ON WRITING

The Political Studies Association (PSA) in the UK has published a useful introductory leaflet entitled *Study Politics at Universities in the UK*. The guide has a section on what students will acquire as part of their studies. Under the heading 'Oral and Written Communication' is the following statement on how studying Politics will help you:

Learn how to discuss and argue from an informed point of view. Ask pertinent questions and sort the important points from the less relevant ones. Learn how to make presentations and develop your skills in summarising arguments and key points. Communicate effectively through writing essays, reports and reviews. By studying Politics, you'll gain a whole host of new communication skills. (Fisher and Arthurs 2002)

Despite many years of compulsory schooling, higher education teachers continue to bemoan the deficiencies of their students in some of the basic ingredients of written communication in English. This is not the place to provide a crash course in how to write, but the guidance that follows provides a brief primer on the basic ingredients of writing: words, sentences, punctuation and paragraphs.

Words are clearly the messengers of both written and oral communication, but different words fit different contexts. The language you might use in discussions with friends and relations about everyday events will be different from the language you will use as a student of Politics. This is clearly the case with the specific vocabulary of terms that have special or different meanings in the academic study of Politics. It is also the case that your audience is different (your tutors and fellow students) and therefore communication with them needs to be more formal. One obvious consequence is the need to avoid slang and colloquial terms. It is equally important not to fall into the opposite trap of overusing technical terms and overly long words that result in your writing being full of meaningless jargon. What you need to aim for is formal and informed use of words, but doing so in a way that does not obscure and over-complicate what you are trying to communicate.

In short, you should be aiming to communicate in plain English. The UK Plain English Campaign defines this as 'a message, written with the reader in mind and with the right tone of voice, that is clear and concise.' The Campaign's advice on the use of words is: 'Say exactly what you mean, using the simplest words that fit. This does not necessarily mean only using simple words – just words that the reader will understand' (Plain English Society, 2002).

In discussing the importance of words in communication, we can't avoid the issue of *spelling*. Spelling mistakes create a bad impression, especially when you make mistakes with terms specific to your subject. Please remember the 'a' in the middle of parliament and the 'n' in the middle of government. Use your spellchecker to teach yourself spelling: make a note of the words you keep misspelling and occasionally test yourself on them. The academic writer always has a good dictionary to hand and uses it.

The Campaign for Plain English also places great emphasis on the importance of keeping your *sentences* short. The longer they are, the harder it is to ensure that you have used the correct grammar throughout. If you are building complex relationships, your sentence might have to be long, but after you have written it, go back and see if it can be broken down into at least two sentences. If you tuck too many additional bits of information into a sentence your reader will lose the main thread. Too many short sentences read rather simplistically and fail to develop links and relationships, but the very occasional short, sharp sentence can give a dramatic emphasis. Try varying the length of your sentences.

Another advantage of keeping sentences briefer is that this will minimise the need for complicated *punctuation*. Here are a few basic prompts on this difficult issue:

1. Don't over use *commas*. Use them only for separating out a list of things (but not before the 'and' for the last item, unless this significantly aids comprehension) and descriptors to a main point. Here's an example. 'Following his election victory, Tony Blair's first ministerial appointments were to the Treasury, the Foreign Office and the Home Office.'
2. Use *colons* to start a list and separate the individual items out with *commas*, and groups of items with *semicolons*.
3. Avoid the many pitfalls of *apostrophes*. The most common error is with the use of it's (only use when you might have written 'it is') and its (as in 'the cat ate its food'). Apostrophes are used to show possession and should come before the 's' when the possessor is single (the cat's food) or after the 's' when plural (the cats' food). Avoid contractions in your academic work like don't and can't – write 'do not' and 'cannot'.

The final part of this primer on written communication deals with *paragraphs*. As with sentences, the secret is to keep them short. You can help yourself to do so by remembering the purpose that paragraphs serve. They exist as signposts to the reader by showing when the writer is moving from one main point to another. You need to emphasise this by normally using your first sentence in the paragraph to make the main point that you want to communicate and to use the other sentences to explain and illuminate the main point. For the next main point, start another paragraph. If you don't, the reader might miss that something new is being said. So if you are giving five alternative explanations of a political event, start each with a new paragraph.

APPLICATION OF NUMBER: A SIMPLE TEST OF NUMERACY

Depending which courses you are required to take, or opt for, you may be able to avoid quantitative aspects of studying

Politics. In research terms we use the word *quantitative* to refer to research that draws on numerical data such as statistics derived from an opinion poll or social survey. This is in contrast to *qualitative* research, which centres more on observing and interviewing participants in the political process, and traditionally includes working with existing documents, especially personal ones like diaries and autobiographies.

If numeracy is not your strong point, continuing to avoid it at university is not really the best thing to do. The national statistics on the percentage of the population who are unable to do simple arithmetic calculations is frightening. If you are in this category, then you should see if your university offers support for numeracy as part of your studies and take the opportunity of making a determined attempt to tackle this key skill. Most employers want to see evidence of numeracy, so if you can, get the extra learning on your CV.

Take a look at the following table and if you cannot easily answer the questions then you need to do some serious remedial word! Answers can be found on page 195.

Would you be more likely/less likely to go and vote at your local polling station if you had a chance to vote for a directly elected mayor in your area?

('N' means number)		Totals	Sex		Age			
			Male	Female	18–24	25–34	35–64	65+
Weighted base		(3)	278	260	63	109	254	114
More likely	(N)	288	146	142	42	71	129	46
	(%)	53	(4)	55	67	65	51	40
Less likely	(N)	135	73	62	12	24	61	38
	(%)	25	(4)	24	19	22	24	33
Already have an elected mayor	(N)	17	6	11	2	1	7	8
	(%)	3	(4)	4	3	1	3	7
Don't know/ refused	(N)	99	54	45	7	12	57	22
	(%)	18	(4)	17	11	11	23	20

Source: *The Guardian* opinion poll, fieldwork 19–21 April 2002

1. How many more of the sample questioned were aged 65+ than 18–24?
2. What is strange about the totals in the row for those who answered 'already have an elected mayor'?
3. What is the missing statistic (3) in the total column?
4. What are the missing statistics (4) in the sex column?
5. What fraction of those responding was of the age 18–24 and how can this fraction be reduced?

INFORMATION TECHNOLOGY: BASIC IT CHECK LIST

You cannot have escaped the increasing importance of being skilled in information technology. Universities are at the forefront of IT developments and you should use your time as a student to fully equip yourself with IT skills both to help your learning and also to strengthen your employability after graduating. There should be plenty of opportunities to learn new skills and improve on existing ones.

As a start, consider the following checklist and then show your results to someone who can advise you on where to go to ensure you become confident on all the basic skills listed. This is only a start. What skills would you add to this list for intermediate and more advanced IT skills?

Checklist on basic IT skills (tick the appropriate columns)

IT skill	Very confident	Fairly confident	Not confident
Logging on to your university IT network			
Finding way around keyboard and using mouse			
Finding and opening applications like a word-processor			
Naming, saving and managing files			

Basic word processing: formatting, editing, saving and pasting, spell-checking
Basic spreadsheet entry and calculations
Adding pictures to word-processed document
Making graphs and charts from a spreadsheet and importing into word processor
Using web browser
Getting information from the web
Using e-mail

WORKING WITH OTHERS: ASPECTS OF GROUP WORK

One of the phrases that you are sure to hear repeatedly at university is that 'you need to be an independent learner'. The contrast is made with previous levels of education where learners are seen as dependent on what is provided by their teachers. This distinction is clearly significant but it could be argued that success in higher education is more likely to be achieved through interdependent learning, that is, learning with others, and that this is a better preparation for life after university. Employers, for example, are increasingly looking for those who can be successful team players, who are able to work with others and for future promotion to take on a leadership role within their work groups.

In recognition of this skill, universities are increasingly adding to their assessment strategies requirements for students to work in groups and to collaborate on reports and presentations.

Working with others in group settings may well be the most demanding skill that you will need to develop, and it may well be the most rewarding. There are some references at the end of this chapter to guidance and advice, but four main aspects of group work are briefly considered here.

The first is that of differing roles within the group. You need to decide, for example, what the role is that you want to play. Do you want to be one of the leaders or are you happy to be a follower? What style of leadership is going to work best with your group – democratic, authoritarian, charismatic, and so on? As a student of Politics, you should have particular insight into this! A useful role the group might like to consider is for someone to keep notes of meetings to circulate to members.

The second aspect of group work is to agree at an early stage some ground rules for how the members are going to work together: sharing work loads, keeping in touch (e-mail is best) and respecting each other (be sensitive to issues relating to differences of age, gender and ethnic group membership in the group).

Thirdly, the group needs to agree a work plan based on agreed goals (the steps you need to take to fulfil the group task), target dates, and a time for a practice run if a presentation is involved. You can apply some of the suggestions on time management that follow to the group setting.

The final aspect of working with others is the interpersonal skill needed to deal with difficult situations arising from the dynamics of the group. Almost certainly you will have to face issues arising from personality clashes, conflicting opinions, and non-participation by some members. There are no easy answers here but a useful piece of advice is for the group to concentrate on the issue rather than the individual who may be at odds with the group. If the conflict is resulting in failure to agree, the latter is the issue, not the individuals concerned, and the way out might be to agree to decide on the basis of voting or for individuals to take it in turns to get their way. And if someone is not participating, don't spend precious energy on forcing the person to participate or waste time waiting for the person to show up: work round the problem by sharing out

the undone work and make it clear to tutors that you have had
to do so.

IMPROVING OWN LEARNING AND PERFORMANCE: TIME MANAGEMENT AND REFLECTION

The inclusion of the key skill of improving own learning and
performance is interesting as it provides a bridge between
key and study skills, but more significantly it serves to
emphasise that learning is not confined to school and college.
This idea is summed up in the phrase 'lifelong learning', and
this is seen as essential for the future of twenty-first-century
societies. This key skill is about being aware of your own
strengths and weaknesses in terms of knowledge, understanding and skills, taking responsibility for your personal
development and having the ability to reflect and learn from
experience. Many aspects of this skill have been dealt with in
the previous chapter but one key learning and performance
skill you will certainly need to succeed in is that of managing
your time.

It is tempting to suggest that time management is *the* most
important skill that students need to master. Consider the vast
range of things you need to do as a student: attending classes,
reading and discussing your course work, undertaking assessment tasks. Then there are all the other things that you want
to, or have to, do as a person in your own right: socialising,
sleeping, eating, attending to the needs of your friends and
family and, increasingly, earning money to help reduce the
debt you are accumulating. Only a very small proportion of
your time for all these things is organised for you – you may
have as little as eight hours a week on your timetable. The
other 160 hours are for you to manage.

The key to successful time management is not complicated.
It is about putting yourself in control of your time, rather than
feeling controlled by others. But it is the hardest thing for most
of us to do. You have to try, however, and no one can do it for
you. You can make a start by continually working on the three

precepts of time management: *Reflecting, prioritising* and *planning*.

Reflecting in this context is about thinking about and analysing what you are doing as a student, why you are doing it, and considering how you might do better at what you are doing. Are you clear about your reasons for coming to university and your longer-term goals? What is more important to you: getting a good degree or having a good time socially? What are you doing that does not really fit in with your goals? Are there some things that you are doing that you don't really need to do? Are there some things that are important to you that you keep putting off? The self-questioning is endless, but if you can't do this as a student, when will you ever do so?

Prioritising is a concrete way of putting reflection into practice. It is almost certain that you won't have time to do everything you want to do or is expected of you by your tutors and other people. Some things will have to go or be put to one side. So you need to identify those things that need to be high priorities and others that can be low priorities. In thinking of the high priorities it is sometimes helpful to distinguish between what is urgent and what is important. Things that are urgent are probably so because they are about tasks and deadlines set by other people. Whether they are important depends on your personal goals and also the impact on you if the deadlines are not met. It is often difficult to prioritise the important over the urgent, but you should seek to do so.

There is no real alternative when prioritising to making lists. Try it out. For the coming week list all the things that you need to find time for. Then try and put them into priority order: most important first, then most urgent, and so on down to least important and urgent. Are there some things at the bottom of the list that can be dispensed with? Computer programs like Microsoft's Outlook have built-in 'To Do' facilities that allow you to assign different levels of priority. Try using one.

Having determined your priorities, the next step is *planning* your time, allocating the time available to complete all the tasks you have prioritised for that day, week or month. For some things you will need to plan further ahead and this applies especially to planning your time for the preparation and completion of assessed work. Look back to the section on organising your learning in the previous chapter.

OK, let's accept that all this time management advice is great in theory but life isn't really like that. However, the alternative of crisis management is worse. Do you really want to sit up through the night finishing that essay? Do you really want to miss a night out with your friends because you haven't done the reading for tomorrow's seminar? You won't always get it exactly right, but a bit of time management will help you to get the most out of being a student – academically and socially.

PROBLEM-SOLVING

It is helpful to deal with problem-solving last. Problem-solving is about finding solutions; about how to get from one situation to another as efficiently and effectively as possible. Most of this chapter has been about finding solutions to such things as better communications, improving numeracy and working with others; and the previous chapter was largely about solutions for studying Politics successfully. As a student you will constantly need to find solutions to these and other problems – how to write that essay, what to get from that journal article, how to prepare for next week's presentation, what topics to revise for the examination, how best to organise your time, *ad infinitum*. The clear message from the two chapters is that solutions are best found by taking a clear and rational approach. This is summed up by the following diagram.

What this model is trying to portray is that problem-solving is a process of moving rationally from an identification of a problem to an analysis and evaluation of the information gathered relating to the problem, to a decision to act which is then implemented. Finally, the outcome of the actions taken are reviewed to see if the problem could be solved better if it occurs again.

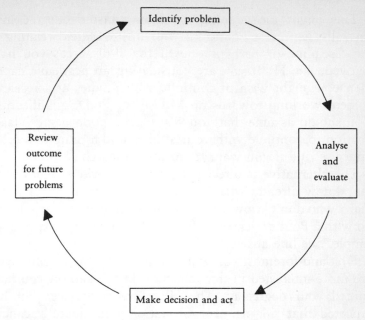

Rational problem-solving model

AFTER YOUR DEGREE: FUTURE STUDIES AND EMPLOYMENT

It is very important that you begin to think as early as possible about what you want to do after you graduate with your Politics degree. Your thoughts on this should influence your choice of option courses and your longer-term aims will help to motivate you to get the best degree result that you can.

A good piece of advice to remember is that it is best not to be too single-minded in your focus on your future employment. Few graduates in the twenty-first century, unlike many of their counterparts in the twentieth century, are likely to enter a lifelong career. Contemporary graduates can expect to have many different jobs during their working life, drawing on the full range of their knowledge and skills and, of course, their continuing lifelong learning achievements.

One clear option – and taken by an increasing number of students – is to continue with your studies.

This might mean doing a taught Master's degree in a specialist aspect of Politics, or moving to a field relating to the discipline or perhaps one of the skills areas you have enjoyed, like IT. If you are considering an academic career then you might wish to continue your studies as a research student working towards an M.Phil. or Ph.D. qualification. You should assume that you will need a good degree classification to continue with your studies and a minimum of an upper second if you want to go into research.

The alternative is direct entry to the world of work. You may know already what you career ambitions are. For the many who don't know, the question is often asked: 'what can I do with a Politics degree?' Hopefully you are not expecting a simple, one-line answer!

First and foremost you will be a graduate. Most employers are more interested in this fact than in the subject you have gained your degree in. The HE Careers Service Unit has reported that 56 per cent of national graduate vacancies between October 2000 and September 2001 were for graduates from any subject. What being a graduate means to employers is that you have proved yourself intellectually and that you have a wide range of study and key skills that are relevant to the world of work. Hopefully, having read this chapter, you will be able to convince an employer of what use you can be to them and give plenty of examples of how your skills are transferable to their organisation.

Second you are a Politics graduate and there are clear employment routes that are particularly suitable given your specialism. Think about the many organisations within the broadly defined 'public sector' that intertwine with governmental and political bodies: the civil service, local authorities, housing associations, the health service, political parties, trade unions and so on. Many administrative and policy jobs in these organisations require their employees to have an understanding of how government works and the impact of the political environment. An interesting area of employment to consider is the 'lobby industry', those whose job it is to organise pressure on international, national and local governments.

You also need to consider those jobs that normally require a professional qualification. Good examples here of relevance to Politics graduates are journalism, social work and teaching (where the introduction of Citizenship on the National Curriculum is likely to open up new and interesting possibilities).

To get more help and advice on employment opportunities, do contact your university careers service. They will have significant experience of supporting Politics graduates and a wealth of resources to share with you. And remember, contact them early on in your degree studies.

One last thought about Politics, skills and employment. There is always the opportunity to put your knowledge of Politics and the skills you have gained into practice by becoming a politician. Not many Politics graduates make a career out of being a politician (but there are some notable examples). Let's face it, there are few opportunities for doing this and getting paid. But many Politics graduates are active on a voluntary basis in political parties, pressure groups and related organisations.

Do you think you could use your understanding of concepts (like **power** and influence), political structures and how governmental institutions work to make a difference, locally, nationally or internationally?

ANSWERS TO QUESTIONS ON PAGE 187 ON NUMERACY

1. $114 - 63 = 51$
2. Total respondents is given as 17 but the totals of those broken down by age for this response is given as 18!
3. $278 + 260 = 538$ (but the answer is 540 if you add up the age figures).
4. 146 as a percentage of 278 is 52%, 73 out of 278 is 26%, the 6 males already having an elected mayor are 2% of all males, and 19% of males didn't know or refused to answer.
5. 42 out of 288 of the women respondents were aged 18–24, so the fraction is expressed as 42/288. This can

be reduced to 7/48 by dividing the top and bottom of
the original fraction by 2 and then by 6.

FURTHER READING

There is a wealth of material in university libraries on key
skills and the following is just a selection of some of the most
useful sources available. The best starting point for further
reading is to consult the recommended reading in Sue Drew
and Rose Bingham's *The Student Skills Guide* (1997). The
Department for Education and Skills is strongly promoting
key skills (it is now in the title of the Department!) and its
website has much useful content and links to other resources
(http://www.dfes.gov.uk/).

Adair, John (1997) *Decision Making and Problem Solving*. London: Institute of
    Personnel and Development.
Bransford, John D. and Barry S. Stein (1993) *The Ideal Problem Solver: A Guide for
    Improving Thinking*. New York: W. H. Freeman.
Cuba, Lee and John Cocking (1994) *How to Write About the Social Sciences*.
    London: HarperCollins.
Drew, Sue and Rose Bingham (1997) *The Student Skills Guide*. Aldershot: Gower.
Fisher, Justin and Jack Arthurs, eds (2002) *Study Politics at Universities in the UK*.
    London: Political Studies Association.
Gaulter, Brian and Lesley Buchanan (1994) *Application of Number*. Oxford: Oxford
    University Press.
Hartley, Peter (1997) *Group Communication*. London: Routledge.
Lewis, Roger (1994) *How to Manage Your Study Time*. London: Collins.
Plain English Society [online] URL: http://www.plainenglish.co.uk/
QAA (2002) [online] URL: http://www.qaa.ac.uk/crntwork/benchmark/
    politics_textonly.html
Rogerson, Simon et al (1995) *Successful Group Work*. London: Kogan Page
Winter, Jonathan (1995) *Skills for Graduates in the 21st Century*. London: Associa-
    tion of Graduate Recruiters.

GLOSSARY

Anarchism An ideology that seeks to end the state's exploitation of individuals. States are to be replaced with spontaneous voluntary associations, free from coercion.

Authority Often defined as legitimate power. It could be argued, however, that the authority of all states rests in practice upon a combination of legitimacy and force.

Balance of power The attempt to reach an equilibrium of power between states in order to maintain international stability.

Capitalist societies Societies whose economies are based upon free market economics and in particular production for profit and the private ownership of property.

Civil society Those political organisations found between the family and the state that enjoy varying degrees of autonomy from the state (these include interests groups, business corporations, media groups, voluntary associations, social clubs and so on).

Class consciousness A Marxist term that refers to a sense of common purpose amongst a social class, the members of which share a particular socio-economic relationship to the mode of production.

Command economy An economy controlled and directed by the state, rather than being left to the free market.

Communism In theory, an egalitarian, classless and stateless social and economic system founded on the collective ownership of the means of production.

Comparative Government An approach to political analysis that examines the similarities and differences between political systems around the world.

Conservatism An ideology that advocates respecting traditional institutions and customs, seeking gradual change rather than revolutionary reform based on untested theoretical principles.

Constitution The source, often consisting of one document, that outlines the over-arching rules of society and the regulations of a territory's political system.

Dark Ages A period of relative intellectual and artistic stagnation in European history (c. 500–1000 AD), which began with the collapse of the classical civilisations of Greece and Rome and ended with the development of medieval society.

Democracy Literally, rule of the people. More often used to signify majority rule through representative government.

Democratic-elitism A variation on classical elite theory which suggests the best form of governance is one that is run by elites who are elected by the masses.

Diplomacy The art of mitigating or reducing conflict, or promoting cooperation, by the means of persuasion or compromise.

Elite theory The school of thought that argues that all political systems are characterised by two groups: the governors and the governed.

Empirical case study The use of real events and evidence to test a theoretical hypothesis.

Environmentalism An ideology that seeks a better balance between man and nature, where the environment is protected and conserved for future generations.

Equality Even-handed treatment avoiding the favouring of certain individuals, groups or classes.

Executive branch The division of government charged with implementing laws.

Faction A small, tightly connected political grouping that is organised to promote the common interests of its members.

False consciousness The belief that a particular set of political, social and economic arrangements work in one's interest when in fact the opposite is true.

Feminism An ideology that seeks to redress the power imbalance between men and women.

Free market An economic ideal whereby the economy runs itself through the laws of supply and demand rather than being planned and directed by government.

French Revolution A pivotal event in the history of politics that began with the overthrow of the monarchy in France in 1789. By establishing a constitution based largely on liberal principles, the revolutionaries helped to popularise and redefine important political concepts such as liberty, equality and nationalism.

Globalisation The growing interdependence of peoples, cultures and economies.

Governance The resolution of social order and distribution of resources at a societal level through the making and enforcing of binding rules.

Government The sub-discipline of Politics that studies domestic public institutions, social groups and movements that determine the rules of, and the distribution of resources within, society.

Idealist school A school of International Relations that seeks to reduce conflict in the world through establishing respected international organisations and international law.

Ideology A lifeguiding system of beliefs, values and goals affecting political style and action.

Interest groups Movements operating from within civil society that seek to influence policy and public opinion but which do not put forward candidates for public office.

Intergovernmental organisations International institutions that are established by, and represent, individual member states.

International Relations The sub-discipline of Politics that studies interaction between, and amongst, states and other international non-state actors.

International society The idea that the commonly agreed laws and institutions that underpin domestic societies can be emulated to form a single world society within the international system.

International system The common structure that houses all the sovereign states and non-state actors engaged in international relations.

Judicial branch The division of government charged with upholding the law.

Justice The provision of a fair balance. Often linked to equality.

Legislative branch The division of government that makes law.

Legitimacy Where a power gains the acceptance of those it governs.

Liberalism An ideology based on the freedom of the individual involving limited government, individual rights, toleration of other views and the free market.

Liberty Lack of constraint allowing the freedom of thought and action.

Limited government A system of government where a degree of sovereignty is reserved for the people, preventing state institutions from violating a citizen's individual freedoms.

Lobbyists Individuals whose profession it is to engage with decision makers, seeking to influence public policy.

Marxism The school of thought, developed by Karl Marx and his successors, that provides a critique of capitalism, highlighting its exploitative nature, and advocates revolutionary activities to precipitate communism.

Methodology Refers to the various conceptual and empirical tools that are used to analyse political and social behaviour. Examples include theoretical perspectives such as feminism and Marxism and research techniques such as data collection, surveys and textual analysis.

Mode of production The dominant system of economic production within a society. Examples include capitalism, feudalism and socialism.

Modules The individual component parts of university degree courses.

Nationalism The desire to bring statehood, its institutions and legal status to a nation.

Natural rights A doctrine associated with early liberals such as John Locke which assumes that all human beings, by mere virtue of existence, possess indivisible basic rights such as life, liberty and property.

Neo-liberalism A term used to describe the ideas of theorists such as Friedrich Hayek whose advocacy of the free market and limited government have strongly influenced governments in countries such as the UK and USA since the late 1970s.

New World Order A term used to describe the international political system in the period after the end of the cold war.

Normative theory Philosophical questions about what ought to be, rather than what actually is.

Obligation The legal or moral requirement that citizens obey the state. Obligation has, at various times in history, been based on the state's ability to provide God's will, security, the public good, and social and economic welfare.

Oligarchy Rule by the few over the many.

Patriarchy A concept popularised by feminism that refers to any social system that is dominated by men.

Pluralist state Where power is divided amongst several competing locations within society.

Pluralists Social scientists who see 'advanced' Western societies as being characterised by a great diversity of beliefs, values and cultural practices.

Policy Analysis An approach to studying Politics that concentrates on the decision making process, in particular institutional interactions, policy inputs and policy outcomes.

Political agenda Whatever social and economic questions are considered by the powerful to be worthy of public debate and eventually perhaps legislative action by political institutions.

Political economy Encompasses in its contemporary meaning various (often competing) approaches to the study of politics (for example, Marxism and rational choice theory), all of which acknowledge in some way or other the interconnected relationships between economic and political processes and institutions.

Political participation Where individual citizens engage with, and seek to influence, the political process.

Political Theory The sub-discipline of Politics that involves the largely abstract critical study of the motivations, values, beliefs and principles that lie behind political behaviour.

Political Sociology An approach found in Political Science and Sociology that places special emphasis upon analysing the relationship between the state and civil society and the connections between political processes and social structures such as class, gender and 'race'.

Postmodernism A recently influential approach to Politics and society that advocates deep scepticism about the 'truth' claims of all ideologies and about rationality generally.

Power The ability to achieve one's objectives even in the face of opposition. Methods used to exercise power include force, persuasion and manipulation.

Proportional representation An electoral system that seeks, in its purest form, to allocate political influence in direct proportion to the number of votes cast for a particular political party.

Protest A display of dissent against a decision or policy.

Public Administration An approach to studying Politics that focuses on the state's institutions.

Public policy The outcome of the political process: a society's laws and their implementation.

Radical school Marxist and neo-Marxist scholars who believe international relations are dominated by economic considerations that largely benefit class, rather than the national, interest.

Realist school Those IR scholars who advocate working within the limitations of the anarchic international system. They see little chance of creating 'world government', and thus suggest the best way for a country to ensure its own security and influence is to maximise its power in relation to other states.

Rights The legal or moral recognition of choice and liberty.

Rule of law The governing of a society through the rational application and enforcement of legislated constraints upon individuals' behaviour. In theory, no one is above the law and all who live under it must have the opportunity to utilise it to protect their interests, where those interests are considered legal.

Scientism The belief that only through the application of scientific methods can we understand human behaviour.

Scrutiny The act of holding public office holders to account.

Separation of the powers The division of sovereignty between the people and the state, and between different branches of government within the state itself.

Social contract A liberal idea that seeks to explain why we obey the state in terms of the consent of the governed via an explicit or (more likely) implicit contract with the sovereign.

Social rights Legal or moral dispensations guaranteeing access to social and economic resources.

Socialism An ideology that seeks social, not private, control over the means of production and distribution in order to guarantee equality.

Sovereignty The supreme source of political authority, subject to no higher power.

State A set of tightly connected governmental institutions, concerned with the administration of a geographically determined population over which the state claims compulsory and universal jurisdiction.

State sovereignty The recognition of the independence, territorial integrity, and inviolability of a state.

Strategic Studies The sub-branch of International Relations that specialises in how states use coercion and violence against one another.

Structural approach An approach to studying Politics that looks at societal influences on the political process.

Supranational organisation Where member states give away some of their sovereignty to an international institution, resulting in the agreements reached by this institution being superior to that of the member states' own national laws.

Totalitarian state Where the state monopolises power within society, controlling political and economic activity through its own institutions, justifying this centralisation through a dominant ideology.

Trade Union Congress An umbrella organisation that embraces most trade unions in the UK.

Transnational corporations Businesses that operate in more than one state economy. The largest of these have created complex networks of foreign subsidiaries across the globe. Also known as multinational corporations.

Treaty of Westphalia A treaty signed in 1648 that established the right of a territory's sovereign to determine that country's religion. From this treaty, the concept of state sovereignty grew, where states are granted unfettered control over their own domestic jurisdiction.

Underdevelopment A school of thought promoting the idea that Western economic prosperity has been achieved at the expense of exploitation and the impoverishment of the peripheral economies in the Third World.

War Armed conflict between two or more political units.

Welfare state A state that redistributes wealth in order to provide basic education, health care and other social services for all its citizens.

World Bank A financial organisation established in the postwar period which has as its main objective the promotion of economic development in the poorest countries of the world.

World Trade Organisation A regulatory body established in 1994 to monitor trade agreements and arbitrate when trade disputes arise.

REFERENCES

Adair, John (1997) *Decision Making and Problem Solving*. London: Institute of Personnel and Development.

Albrow, Martin (1996) *The Global Age*. Cambridge: Polity Press.

Allison, Graham T. (1971) *Essence of Decision: Explaining the Cuban Missile Crisis*. Boston: Little, Brown.

Anderson, Benedict (1983) *Imagined Communities*. London: Verso.

Anderson, Peter J. (1996) *The Global Politics of Power, Justice and Death: An Introduction to International Relations*. London: Routledge.

Aristotle [c. 335–323 BC] (1962) *The Politics*. London: Penguin.

Atkinson, Brian, Barry McCarthy and Ken Phillips (1987) *Studying Society. An Introduction to Social Science*. Oxford: Oxford University Press.

Ball, Alan and Guy Peters (2000) *Modern Government and Politics* (sixth edition), Basingstoke: Macmillan.

Ball, Terence (1995) *Reappraising Political Theory*. Oxford: Clarendon Press.

Barrass, Robert (1984) *A Guide to Effective Study, Revision and Examination Techniques*. London: Chapman Hall.

BBC (1995) *From Plato to Nato*. Harmondsworth: Penguin.

Bealey, Frank, Richard Chapman and Michael Sheehan (1999) *Elements in Political Science*. Edinburgh: Edinburgh University Press.

Berridge, Geoff (2002) *Diplomacy: Theory and Practice* (second edition). Basingstoke: Palgrave.

Blondel, Jean (1981) *The Discipline of Politics*. London: Butterworths.

Bottomore, Tom (1993) *Political Sociology* (second edition). London: Pluto Press.

Bottomore, Tom (1993a) *Elites and Society* (second edition). London: Pluto Press.

Bourner, Tom and Phil Race (1995) *How to Win as a Part-time Student: A Study Skills Guide*. London: Kogan Page.

Bransford, John D. and Barry S. Stein (1993). *The Ideal Problem Solver: A Guide for Improving Thinking*. New York: W. H. Freeman.

Bryson, Valerie (1992) *Feminist Political Thought: an Introduction*. Basingstoke: Macmillan.

Bull, Hedley (2002) *The Anarchical Society* (third edition). Basingstoke: Palgrave.

Burke, Edmund, [1790] (1968) *Reflections on the Revolution in France*. London: Penguin.

Buxton, William (1998) *Talcott Parsons and the Capitalist Nation-state: Political Sociology as a Strategic Vocation*. Toronto: University of Toronto Press.

Buzan, Barry (1987) *An Introduction to Strategic Studies*. Basingstoke: Macmillan.

Callinicos, Alex (1984) 'Marxism and politics' In Leftwich, Adrian, ed. (1984), pp. 124–38.

Calvocoressi, Peter (2000) *World Politics 1945–2002* (eighth edition). London: Longman.

Clapham, Christopher (1985) *Third World Politics: An Introduction*. London: Routledge.

Clausewitz, Carl [1831] (1976) *On War*. Princeton: Princeton University Press.

Clegg, Steven (1989) *Frameworks of Power*. London: Sage.

Coole, Diana (1993) *Women in Political Theory*. London: Harvester Wheatsheaf.

Crème, Phyllis and Mary Lea (1997) *Writing at University: A guide for students*. Buckingham: Open University Press.

Crick, Bernard (2000) *In Defence of Politics* (fifth edition), London: Continuum.

Cuba, Lee and John Cocking (1994) *How to Write About the Social Sciences*. London: HarperCollins.

Dahl, Robert (1961) *Who Governs?*. Chicago: University of Chicago.

Dahl, Robert (1967) *Pluralism and Democracy in the United States*. Chicago: Rand McNally.

Dahl, Robert (1982) *Dilemmas of Pluralist Democracy*. New Haven, CT: Yale University Press.

Dahl, Robert (1957) 'The concept of power'. *Behavioural Sciences* 2(3), pp. 202–3.

Dalton, Russell (1996) *Citizen Politics* (second edition), New Jersey: Chatham House.

Dicken, Peter (1998) *Global Shift* (third edition). London: Paul Chapman.

Drew, Sue and Rose Bingham (1997) *The Student Skills Guide*. Aldershot: Gower.

Dunleavy, Patrick (1986). *Studying for a Degree in the Humanities and Social Sciences*. London: Macmillan.

Dye, Thomas R. and Harmon Zelgler (2000) *The Irony of Democracy: An Uncommon Introduction to American Politics* (eleventh edition). New York: International Thomson Publishing.

Dylan, Bob (1989) *Political World*. Track one from the CBS album *Oh Mercy* (02-465800-10).

Enloe, Cynthia H. (1992) *Bananas, Beaches and Bases: Making Feminist Sense of International Relations*. London: Pandora.

Faulks, Keith (1999) *Political Sociology: A Critical Introduction*. Edinburgh: Edinburgh University Press.

Fisher, Justin and Jack Arthurs, eds (2002). *Study Politics at Universities in the UK*. London: Political Studies Association.

Frank, André Gunder (1969) *Capitalism and Underdevelopment in Latin America*. New York: Modern Reader Paperbacks.

Freeman, Richard (1991) *Mastering Study Skills*. London: Macmillan.

Gamble, Andrew, David Marsh and Tony Tait (1999) *Marxism and Social Science*. Basingstoke: Macmillan.

Gaulter, Brian and Lesley Buchanan (1994) *Application of Number*. Oxford: Oxford University Press.

Giddens, Anthony (1985) *The Nation-state and Violence*. Cambridge: Polity Press.

Gilpin, Robert (2001) *Global Political Economy*. Princeton: Princeton University Press.

Goodwin, Barbara (1997) *Using Political Ideas*. Chichester: John Wiley.

Gowers, Sir Ernest (1987) *The Complete Plain Words*. Harmondsworth: Penguin.

Hague, Rod and Martin Harrop (2001) *Comparative Government and Politics* (fifth edition). Basingstoke: Palgrave.

Hamilton, Alexander, James Madison and John Jay [1787/1788] (1961) *The Federalist Papers*. New York: Mentor.

Hampsher-Monk, Iain (1992) *A History of Modern Political Thought: Major Thinkers from Hobbes to Marx*. Oxford: Blackwell.

Harris, Marvin (1993) *Culture, People, Nature: An Introduction to General Anthroplogy*. London: Harper Collins.

Harrison, Lisa (2001) *Political Research: An Introduction*. London: Routledge.

Hartley, Peter (1997) *Group Communication*. London: Routledge.

Hay, Colin (1997) 'Divided by a common language: political theory and the concept of power', *Politics* 17 (1), pp. 45–52.

Hayek, Friedrich (1944) *The Road to Serfdom*. London: Routledge.

Heywood, Andrew (1998) *Political Ideologies: An Introduction*. Basingstoke: Palgrave.

Heywood, Andrew (1999) *Political Theory: An Introduction* (seciond edition). Basingstoke: Palgrave.

Hitler, Adolf [1925] (1969) *Mein Kampf*. London: Hutchinson.

Hobbes, Thomas [1651] (1968) *Leviathan*. London: Penguin.

Hoffman, John (1995) *Beyond the State*. Cambridge: Polity Press.

Honey, P. and Alan Mumford (1992) *Manual of Learning Styles*. Maidenhead: P. Honey.

Jones, Bill, Dennis Kavanagh, Phillip Norton and Michael Moran (2001) *Politics UK* (fourth edition). Harlow: Longman.

Kavanagh, Dennis (1983) *Political Science and Political Behaviour*. London: Allen and Unwin.

Kingdom, John (1999) *Government and Politics in Britain* (second edition). Oxford: Polity.

Kolakowski, Leszek (1978) *Main Currents of Marxism*, 3. Oxford: Oxford University Press.

Kolb, David A. (1984) *Experimental Learning*. Englewood Cliffs, NJ: Prentice-Hall.

Kuhn, Thomas (1962) *The Structure of Scientific Revolutions*. Chicago: Chicago University Press.

Lasswell, Harold (1936) *Politics: Who Gets What, When, How?*. New York: McGraw-Hill.

Laqueur, Walter (1971) *Dictionary of Politics*. London: Weidenfeld and Nicolson.

Lashley, Conrad (1995) *Improving Study Skills. A Competence Approach*. London: Cassell.

Laver, Michael (1983) *Invitation to Politics*. Oxford: Blackwell.

Lee, James R. (1994) 'The New World Order and the study of international relations: has anything changed?' In: William C. Olson, *Theory and Practice of International Relations*. Englewood Cliffs: Prentice Hall, pp. 28–33.

Leftwich, Adrian (1984) 'On the politics of politics' In Leftwich, Adrian, ed. (1984), pp. 1–18.

Leftwich, Adrian, ed. (1984) *What is Politics?*. Oxford: Blackwell.

Lewis Roger (1994) *How to Manage Your Study Time*. London: Collins.

Locke, John [1690] (1988) *Two Treatises of Government*. Cambridge: Cambridge University Press.

Lukes, Steven (1974) *Power: A Radical View*. London: Macmillan.

Machiavelli, Niccolò [1513] (1981) *The Prince*. Harmondsworth: Penguin.

Mackenzie, William (1967) *Politics and Social Science*. Harmondsworth: Penguin.

Mair, Lucy (1962) *Primitive Government*. Middlesex: Penguin.

Mann, Michael (1986) *The Sources of Social Power*, 1. Cambridge: Cambridge University Press.

Mann, Michael (1993) *The Sources of Social Power*, 2. Cambridge: Cambridge University Press.

Marsh, David and Gerry Stoker, eds (1995) *Theory and Methods in Political Science*. Basingstoke: Palgrave.

Marsh, David and Gerry Stoker (1995) 'Conclusions' In Marsh, David and Gerry Stoker, eds (1995), pp. 288–97.

Marshall, Lorraine and Frances Rowland (1993) *A Guide to Learning Independently* (second edition). Buckingham: Open University Press.

Marx, Karl and Friedrich Engels [1848] (1967) *The Communist Manifesto*. Harmondsworth: Penguin.

Marx, Karl (1875) *Critique of the Gotha Programme* [online] URL: http://www.ex.ac.uk/Projects/meia/Archive/1875–Gotha [Accessed on 4 May 2002].

McKay, David (2001) *American Politics and Society* (fifth edition). Oxford: Blackwell.

Michels, Roberto (1962) *Political parties: A Sociological Study of the Oligarchical Tendencies of Modern Democracies*. New York: Freedom Press.

Mill, John Stuart [1859] (1974) *On Liberty*. London: Penguin.

Minogue, Kenneth (1995) *Politics: A Very Short Introduction*. Oxford: Oxford University Press.

Moodie, Graeme (1984) 'Politics is about government' In Leftwich, Adrian, ed. (1984), pp. 19–32.

Morgan, Alastair (1995) *Improving Your Students' Learning: Reflections on the Experience of Study*. London: Kogan Page.

Morgenthau, Hans (1985) *Politics Among Nations*. New York: Knopf.

Nash, Kate (2000) *Contemporary Political Sociology*. Oxford: Blackwell.

Nicholson, Michael (2002) *International relations: a concise introduction* (second edition). Basingstoke: Palgrave.

Nicholson, Peter (1984) 'Politics and force' In Leftwich, Adrian, ed. (1984), pp. 33–45.

Nietzsche, Friedrich [1886] (1990) *Beyond Good and Evil*. London: Penguin.

Northedge, Andrew (1992) *The Good Study Guide*. Milton Keynes: Open University.

Nozick, Robert (1974) *Anarchy, State and Utopia*. Oxford: Blackwell.

Ohmae, Kenichi (1995) *The End of the Nation-state*. New York: Free Press.

Paine, Thomas [1776] (1995) 'Common sense' In *Rights of Man, Common Sense and Other Political Writings*. Oxford: Oxford University Press.

Pareto, Vilfredo (1968) *The Rise and Fall of the Elites*. New Jersey: Bedminister Press.

Pask, Gordon (1978) 'Styles and strategies of learning' *British Journal of Educational Psychology*, 1976, no. 46, pp. 128–48.

Pateman, Carol (1988) *The Sexual Contract*. Cambridge: Polity Press.

Plain English Society [online] URL: http://www.plainenglish.co.uk/

Plato [c. 380 BC] (1987) *The Republic*. London: Penguin.

QAA (2002) [online] URL: http://www.qaa.ac.uk/crntwork/benchmark/politics_textonly.html

QAA (2002) 'Subject benchmarks statements: politics and international relations' [online] URL: http://www.qaa.ac.uk/crntwork/benchmark/politics%5ftextonly.html [Accessed on 10 December 2002].

Renwick, Alan and Ian Swinburn (1987) *Basic Political Concepts* (second edition). London: Stanley Thornes (Publishers) Ltd.

Roberts, Geoffrey (1971) *Dictionary of Political Analysis*. Harlow: Longman.

Robertson, David (1993) *Penguin Dictionary of Politics*. Harmondsworth: Penguin.

Rogerson, Simon et al (1995) *Successful Group Work*. London: Kogan Page

Root, Michael (1993) *Philosophy of Social Science*. Oxford: Blackwell.

Rosenberg, Justin (1994) *The Empire of Civil Society: A Critique of the Realist Theory of International Relations*. London: Verso.

Rousseau, Jean-Jacques [1762] (1968) *The Social Contract*. Harmondsworth: Penguin.

Rowntree, Derek (1998) *Learn How To Study*. London: Warner Books.

Rush, Michael (1992) *Politics and Society*. London: Harvester Wheatsheaf.

Russett, Bruce, Harvey Starr and David Kinsella (2000) *World Politics: The Menu for Choice* (sixth edition). Boston: Bedford/St Martins.

Sanders, David (1995) 'Behavioural analysis' In Marsh, David and Gerry Stoker, eds (1995), pp. 58–75.

Schedler, Andreas, ed. (1997) *The End of Politics?*. Basingstoke: Macmillan.

Schelling, Thomas C. (1980) *The Strategy of Conflict*. Cambridge, MA: Harvard University Press.

Schumpeter, Joseph A. (1976) *Capitalism, Socialism and Democracy*. London: George Allen and Unwin.

Scruton, Roger (1996) *Dictionary of Political Thought*. London: Pan.

Smith, Adam [1776] (1976) *Wealth of Nations*. Oxford: Clarendon.

Stoker, Gerry (1995) 'Introduction' In Marsh, David and Gerry Stoker, eds (1995), pp. 1–18.

Thomas, Paul (1994) *Alien Politics: Marxist State Theory Retrieved*. London: Routledge.

Thomson, Alex (1996) *Incomplete Engagement: US Foreign Policy Towards South Africa*. Aldershot: Avebury.

Thomson, Alex (2000) *An Introduction to African Politics*. London: Routledge.

Thucydides [c. 420 BC] (1954) *A History of the Peloponnesian Wars*. Harmondsworth: Penguin.

Waltz, Kenneth H. (1979) *Theory of International Politics*. Reading, MA: Addison-Wesley.

Waters, Malcolm (1995) *Globalization*. London: Routledge.

Weber, Max (1948) *From Max Weber: Essays in Sociology*. London: Routledge and Kegan Paul.

Wilson, Woodrow (1899) *The State: Elements of Practical and Political Politics*. London: Isbister.

Winship, Ian and Alison McNab (1998) *The Student's Guide to the Internet 1998*. London: Library Association Publishing.

Winter, Jonathan (1995) *Skills for Graduates in the 21st Century*. London: Association of Graduate Recruiters.

INDEX

207